THE COMPLEX INFRASTRUCTURE KNOWN AS THE FEMALE MIND

The Complex Infrastructure Known as the Female Mind

by Relient K

with Mark Nicholas

TRANSIT

www.TransitBooks.com
A Division of Thomas Nelson, Inc.
www.ThomasNelson.com

Published by W Publishing Group, a Division of Thomas Nelson, Inc., P.O. Box 141000, Nashville, Tennessee, 37214.

W Publishing Group books may be purchased in bulk for educational, business, fundraising, or sales promotional use. For information, please email SpecialMarkets@ThomasNelson.com.

All Scripture quotations, unless otherwise indicated, are taken from The Holy Bible, New International Version (NIV). Copyright © 1973, 1978, 1984. International Bible Society. Used by permission of Zondervan Bible Publishers.

Editorial Staff: Kate Etue (Senior Editor), Lori Jones, Ramona Richards

Cover Design: Margaret Pesek, N•House Design, Nashville, Tennessee

Illustrations: Matt Logan, New York, New York

Published in association with Jeff Risden at Alabaster Arts.

Library of Congress Cataloging-in-Publication Data

The complex infrastructure known as the female mind/by Relient K.
    p. cm.
  ISBN 0-8499-4496-1
    1. Teenage girls—United States. 2. Teenage girls—Psychology. 3. Typology (Psychology)
  4. Teenage boys—Psychology. 5. Interpersonal relations in adolescence. 6. Self-
  acceptance—Religious aspects—Christianity. I. Relient K (Musical group)
  HQ798.C568 2004
  305.235'2—dc22   2004015251

Printed in the United States of America

04 05 06 07 08 PHX 9 8 7 6 5 4 3 2 1

Contents

KiCK OFF: Introduction

I f you are reading this, you might be laughing to yourself and thinking that we have lost our minds. "Relient K writing a book about girls? That's insane." And you would be right. Sort of right, but not really. We might be insane, or we might not—we'll leave that up to you to decide. But for the moment, we won't dwell on the issue of our sanity but on our motivation for undertaking this newest literary pursuit.

So, the other day we got a call from our band's manager, Jeff. Do you know what it's like to have a band manager? Managers have a reputation for being the bearer of either great or horrible news. A phone call from a manager could go something like this: "Hey, guys, you are going to be on the cover of *AP* next month . . . (which would be completely rad) or "Hey, guys, your spring tour just got cancelled because of low ticket sales, so you might want to think about that pizza delivery job at Papa John's . . . (which also hasn't happened yet, thankfully). So when the phone rings and it's your manager, your stomach is in knots because you just don't know what is coming next.

In this case, Jeff was calling with neither great nor horrible news. His news was interesting, to say the least, or maybe even a bit weird. "Hey, guys, I got a call from Thomas Nelson. You know, the big book publisher. Uh huh, that's right. They were calling me to see if you would be interested in writing a book." (Silence.) "Yes, a book." (More silence.) "What's it about? Well . . . um, they want you to write a book about girls." (Again, silence.) "Hello? Are you there?" And that is how this all began—with one simple phone call from our manager.

Now it should be said that we have never been asked to write a book before. In fact, none of us has ever even tried to write a book before. Songs? Obviously. Books? No. But the idea of writing a book sounded like a bit of a challenge, and if there's one thing that you should know about Relient K, it is that we're always up to try something new and we're not ones to turn our backs on a challenge. Besides, how do you turn down an offer to write a book? In our case, you don't.

While writing a book about girls sounded like fun, none of us really had the time to sit down and write the whole thing up. Generally speaking, we're fairly busy. If we aren't on tour, or writing songs, or recording songs for a new record, we are spending our few remaining days at home with friends and family. Quite frankly, even though we wanted to write this book, we weren't sure how we were going to do it. That's where Mark comes in. The editor at Thomas Nelson suggested a guy who she thought would be able to help us out. Unlike us, he had written a book before. So we had our manager Jeff meet with him, and he reported back that he seemed like a decent enough guy, so we invited him in to help us out with this book. For the purposes of this book, he will be like the fifth member of the band. No, he doesn't play an instrument (except the tuba and trombone, but those are barely instruments and they certainly don't count as we're not a ska or a polka band), so you will never see him onstage with us. Think of him as the guy in the back of the van that types on his laptop all day long. So that there is a little "behind the scenes" info for you on why we are writing this book. Basically, we are writing this book because we were asked, and because, with a little extra help, we could.

The other question you may be asking yourself is *Are these guys* qualified *to write a book about girls?* Now that is a fair question, but it will seem almost silly when you stop and think about it. Between the five of us, we have spent the better part of our lives studying and trying to get to know you girls—all different types of girls. That comes to over one hundred years experience when you add it all up.

Secondly, we like girls. We've met plenty of girls, we've hung out with girls, we've dated girls, and a couple of us have even been so lucky as to marry girls. But we won't pretend that we have completely figured out the entire mystery that makes up the female gender. What we *have* discovered in our one-hundred-plus years is that the more we studied your gender, the more complex you and your world became. Your world is and shall remain *The Complex Infrastructure Known as the Female Mind.*

So this is a book about girls, written by some guys who like girls and have observed girls in their natural habitats. We have studied you and your kind for some time now, and at present we are ready to share what we have learned about you, The Girl. This is a Relient K exposé, if you will. An attempt to get to the bottom of what types of girls exist and what makes you tick. Some of it may surprise you, and some of it you probably already know.

If you are a female and are reading this book, you may be thinking quietly to yourself that you surely must know everything there is to possibly know about being a female, because you are one. Oh, contraire, dear girl friend. Even if you know everything there is to know about your own type of girl, remember that there are other girls of other types that you may know very little about. Those other girls may be wildly different than you. If you are the least bit curious about these other kinds of girls, this book is written with you in mind, the complex female. If you are still doubtful that this book is for you, we cordially invite you to take a little test to see if you should indeed be reading this book.

Normally, you won't find a quiz in the introduction of any old book, but you certainly got your money's worth with this book, didn't you? So in order to make sure our quiz works properly and will provide you with the most helpful information that you can stand, there is only one ground rule: Honesty. If you answer the questions with a little honesty, then you will discover if you must continue reading this book or whether to put it down and forget it even existed.

Here's the quiz:

1. Have you ever in your entire life wondered what a boy was thinking?
2. Have you ever felt like you don't know where you fit in?
3. Have you ever felt strangely drawn to the bathroom mirror but didn't know why?
4. Do you ever wonder how some girl could possibly be so popular while others aren't?
5. Do you want to know why it takes a girl longer to get ready for school than a guy?
6. Do you know what the #1 rated drink of girls in America is?
7. Do you own one or more Relient K albums?
8. Have you ever cried during a movie?
9. Are all airheads dumb?
10. Do you like boys?

Would you like to see how you did?

Answers: 1. Yes 2. Yes 3. Yes 4. Yes 5. Yes 6. Diet Coke 7. Yes 8. Yes
9. No 10. Yes

If you answered more than four of these questions correctly (and
honestly), this book is for you.

For the Guys

To those of us on the XY chromosome side of the table, girls are an
enigma, a riddle, and a varied mess of makeup and emotion—not
easily understood, but instead are feared and admired from a safe distance. If you are a guy and happen to be reading this book, good for
you. Once you are finished, you will have all the inside knowledge
about the opposite sex that you have ever wished to know, or at least
everything that we ourselves know.

Most males are a bit afraid of the female gender and how her mind
works. Most times, we just don't understand the ladies. Normally, the
things that we don't understand, we run away from and instead talk of
football, pro wrestling, and music amongst ourselves. That is the stuff
we readily understand. But today is different. Today we will valiantly
attempt to uncover and explain the mystery, the beauty, the behaviors,
and the assortment that make up the female gender. Since girls come in
a wide variety of colors, shapes, and sizes, we will make an effort to clas-
sify them all into easy-to-identify groups, tell you more about their individual habits, their likes and dislikes, and maybe even make it easier for
you to get to know them. They are, after all, the fairer sex and, as a rule,
a far more lovely gender than that of our own. Wouldn't you like to get
to know a girl, even talk to her? We hope that by the time this book is
done, you too will be able to hold a conversation with a girl, spend time
with a girl, and even know how to treat and care for her.

Disclaimer: Remember, as you read about the wild and wonderful
world of girls, not all girl types, guy types, or relationship types are

set in stone. There will be plenty of mixing and matching along the way. This may require your thinking caps. Have them handy, just in case. But don't worry, it will all become apparent later in this book. Clearly, this is an important work of scientific research and unmitigated fact and in some cases, pure conjecture. Pulitzer Prize, here we come (and, yes, we all just rolled our eyes, too . . .)

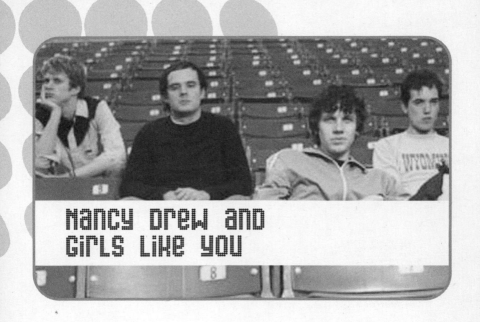

NANCY DREW AND
GIRLS LIKE YOU

Girl Types

THe AtHLete

ou know this person instantly upon sight or sound. Hearing the signature whiff whiff whiff of smooth Polyester/Lycra blend or the faint metallic clink of a dozen pant leg snaps should provide some clue. Seeing the three-stripe black or navy blue Adidas warm-up suit with the high, tightly pulled ponytail is an immediate, dead giveaway. Meet The Athlete. The Athlete participates in a minimum of three sports, usually consisting of volleyball (in the fall), basketball (in the winter), and soccer (in the spring). She may, however, participate in cross-country, swimming, and track & field. Please know that tennis and softball participants are usually not Athletes and play these sports as a hobby or on a recreational basis. Girls who play golf are never Athletes. Golf is not a sport.

Sometimes Workout Girl is mistaken for The Athlete, but they are two completely different people. The Work Out Girl drinks designer bottled water, attends Pilates class, and wears makeup when she does. She likes to wear matching workout gear and has a cute yoga mat that matches her cute yoga pants and top. She likes yoga because she doesn't have to get all sweaty and icky—and she can still look good with her makeup on. The Athlete has little patience for Work Out Girl. They have nothing in common and are not friends.

The Athlete is a high-spirited and competitive girl who likes to hang out with boys as much or more so than girls. We think that's cool. In fact, though she may enjoy hanging out with boys, The Athlete is always secretly trying to beat the boys in anything and everything. For instance, if she is mountain biking, her primary objective is, if not to keep up with the boys, to beat the boys in pedaling up a strenuous and treacherous trail. If she does, she is careful not to smirk, and she doesn't gloat but smiles to herself and basks in the glow of her victory. She loves to surpass boys in all their testosteroned glory. This is among her proudest moments and even guys seem to like a girl who can beat them at their own game. Why guys seem to be drawn to a girl who can show them up, we have no idea, but they do.

The Athlete craves the test, the competition, and the game. She is drawn to any sort of competition—like an upset child's ice cream cone is drawn to a sidewalk on a hot summer day. She is forever making a sport out of mundane things, like racing to finish lunch first, finishing her homework first, or doing pretty much anything first. The Athlete also enjoys sinking wadded notebook paper balls from long distances into trashcans. Though a bored *male* basketball player originally developed this particular non-sport in the mid 1960s, it has, in recent years, become quite popular with the bored female Athlete.

The Athlete is outgoing and personable and cool to be around. She is also funny and quick-witted. This might well be caused by the increased oxygen flow to her brain as she runs all over the place. However, this is just a guess, as oxygen=funniness is not a scientifically proven fact. Her funniness and fun-ness are pretty much constant, unless she has recently been defeated in a match, game, or other competitive act. If this happens, The Athlete is given over to a period of sullenness or mild depression. Don't worry. This will pass quickly because The Athlete will soon realize that there's always another act of competition to get psyched up for.

We have already touched on The Athlete's attire. It is a hard and fast rule that she prefers wearing windbreakers and other non-natural fibered clothing. You will never see her in a dress (not even at church), but she will wear a dress to prom, or so we're told. The Athlete's preferred method of hair styling is to fix her hair in a ponytail at the top and back of her head, WET, within the first 3 minutes of leaving the shower. This way there is no need for a hair dryer or any other hair

> **THE ATHLETE IN 5 WORDS OR LESS:**
> disciplined
> competitive
> nice
> confident
> outgoing

device, and she can quickly get on with other competitive acts—like seeing how fast she can get dressed and out the front door on her way to school. (The Athlete's mother is always worried that her precious daughter will catch "her death of cold" because of her "wet head." The Athlete is the only type of girl to wander outside in the middle of winter with a "wet head." It is important to note that she never *does* catch "her death of cold.")

We should also mention that, although many Athletes attempt this fashion faux pas, the sports bra is not a Relient K-approved top to be worn out in public by The Athlete. It should be worn in conjunction with and under an approved shirt, like a Relient K hooded sweatshirt, which is a smart accessory for any soccer practice. Unless you are Brandi Chastain and have just won the 1999 Women's World Cup in soccer, there are no exemptions to this rule.

The Athlete always wears a rubber sports watch. It's always the kind that can go underwater to like 100 meters—'cause you never know when water polo may go DEEP. The Athlete will often use her sports watch to time herself while doing a variety of things. She always wants to see if she can beat her previous time. If there is no one else around to beat, she will always try to beat herself. Because of this, The Athlete is also a good student. She consistently will try and outdo her previous accomplishments. So don't be surprised to see The Athlete on the Honor Roll.

The Athlete is usually fairly popular. She is well known throughout the school, especially with her fellow athletes. This is fairly typical of athletes in general because they are the primary participants of spectator sports. People show up to watch them compete and thus know who they are. If she happens to be really good at one or more of her sports and lives in a smaller town, she is probably well known throughout the town. Folks at the post office or the grocery store are prone to talk about the successful Athlete and her latest game or match victory. What else is there to talk about in a small town? If she is a super good athlete and, say, wins the state title in the 1000m race, she may even be the Grand Marshal of that town's Fourth of July parade and be given the key to the city by the mayor. But that's only in a very small town. Even though most people know who she is, The Athlete usually has a smaller, close-knit circle of friends. Her friends tend to be other Athletes and that's no surprise. Of course, they might have a few friends that aren't big sports people, but no one knows The Athlete's life of working out, training, and competing like another fellow Athlete.

If you are beginning to think that The Athlete has no problems and her life is great, you are mistaken. The Athlete finds it hard to communicate her true feelings to others around her. Other people see her for what she most obviously is and that is The Athlete—the confident, outgoing, talented, sports-loving person and those are the things that most people relate to her about. Even with her fellow athletes, sports are the dominant theme of any conversation. But there is a whole other side to her that goes unnoticed. The Athlete wishes she fit in better with the girls and that boys see her more as a girl than a buddy. Guys tend to like to hang around The Athlete and think of her as more of a brother than as a girl. While she likes the challenge of competing with the boys, in her heart she would much rather be considered a girl (lady) who the boys like and find attractive and mysterious, instead of getting punched in the arm by them. And she feels that she is at some distance from other girls, too. Most non-Athlete girls don't identify much with all the sports and sweat and stuff that are so much a part of her life. It takes a lot of work for The Athlete and the non-athlete girl to find some common ground and to become friends. She can become trapped in a world of sports, and The Athlete has a hard time communicating her true feelings.

The Athlete likes church just fine, and especially the monthly youth group outings to play miniature golf, go cart racing, or bowling. This means competition. Since there is always an abundance of pizza at youth group functions, she may bring her own brown bag meal complete with energy bars and sports drink. Pizza slows her down and makes her feel sluggish. She doesn't like that feeling, as she never knows when she will need to be up and ready for a footrace (against a boy) in the parking lot. She does, however, have to give in once in a while for the occasional slice . . . because as we all know, "everybody loves pizza." It almost goes without saying that her favorite Bible verse is "run the race to win" (1 Corinthians 9:24). She tends to make that her life's goal and ambition. She also loves the FCA meetings at school and may even be the president.

5 CLUES THAT YOU MIGHT BE THE ATHLETE:

1. You own one dress that your mom made you buy for your cousin's wedding.

2. You stop by the gas station every morning before school to pick up some Gatorade and Powerbars.

3. Your wristwatch has a stopwatch and heart rate monitor and is waterproof.

4. You don't own any shirts with buttons.

5. You have never used a fake doctor's excuse or note from your parent to get out of gym class.

WHAT WOULD YOU FIND IN HER LOCKER? Cleats, an old ace bandage, athletic tape (but no pre-wrap 'cause pre-wrap is for wusses), gym bag, picture of Mia Hamm, empty water bottles

FAVORITE MAGAZINES: SI, *Basketball Digest*, *Runner's World*

EMAIL SIGNATURE: "Strength does not come from physical capacity. It comes from an indomitable will."
—Mahatma Gandhi

FAVORITE MOVIE: Bend It Like Beckham

FAVORITE MUSIC: Melanie C (aka Sporty Spice's sad solo career), Jock Jams, The Chicago Bulls' theme song

TV CHANNEL OR SHOW: ESPN Sports Center

FAVORITE DRINK: Red Bull

SHOES: New Balance Cross trainers

WEBSITE: http://www.womenssportsfoundation.org/

PICTURE/POSTERS: David Beckham

PROBABLE NICKNAMES: Killer or Spike

AFTER SCHOOL JOB: Practice, practice, practice

CLOTHING LABEL: Tie between Adidas and Nike

MAKEUP: no

DID YOU KNOW . . . ? She sleeps in her uniform before a big game for good luck. (And guess who doesn't wash her socks for the same reason?)

Brian Pittman on
THE ATHLETE:

I knew this girl named Julia. Once we hit junior high, Julia started to stand out. I was just glad to finally make it up to what seemed like the real world. People started to develop their own personalities. A lot of the girls were out buying all the latest clothes, but she seemed to be very comfortable in her sweatpants, proudly wearing her basketball #22 jersey wherever possible. As the year went on, she was always the one to wear the school colors and she never seemed to run out of Perry High School clothes. With each season came a new sport, and Julia seemed to love every single one of them. I got to know her through the years, and I run into her at home every once in a while. Last time I saw her she was wearing her senior basketball hooded sweatshirt and black sweatpants. I was glad to see she was still at it.

THE ROCK CHICK

f you happen to be looking down at the ground and spot a pair of black Chuck Taylors worn by a girl, there is an 80 percent chance that you have successfully identified a Rock Chick. If your sleuthing abilities prove correct, there is a 93 percent chance that she is also looking at the ground, because that is what Rock Chicks often do (otherwise known as "shoe gazing"). Another way to quickly identify a Rock Chick: they tend to change their hair color on a weekly or bi-weekly basis. They usually attempt this feat all by themselves or at the hands of another like-minded Rock Chick.

It is a bit tricky to describe to you the methodology with which The Rock Chick chooses and changes her hair color, but we will attempt to shed light on this tricky, hairy subject. First The Rock Chick must start with fairly short hair—no longer than shoulder length but usually stopping mid-neck. Next, it is blunt cut to one length all over or she might choose to have straight bangs cut two thirds of the way up between her eyebrows and her hairline. This is the preferred haircut of The Rock Chick. Next comes the color. The Rock Chick starts with a base color of either black or really, really blond (nearly white). Black is the preferred color for most Rock Chicks. You will not see a true Rock Chick with brown hair. This is unthinkable and must be avoided at all costs. Next she will choose a color for the week. This color is then applied to select sections of her hair in a highlighted fashion. There is a basic color pallet for these highlights that all Rock Chicks stick to. In order of popularity, the highlight pallet colors are brick red, followed closely by hot pink. From there you have your royal blue, then purple, followed by a striking canary yellow or burnt orange. Green comes next, but most Rock Chicks realize that it is an unflattering color. The more serious, or hard core, Rock Chick may even reverse this coloring process and start with a base color of red, pink, blue, purple, yellow, or burnt orange and then go with black or blond highlights. Are you still with us?

Moving right along to other visual identifiers for The Rock Chick, we come next to her makeup. Some Rock Chicks wear makeup and others not at all. Those who do wear makeup prefer black eyeliner and ruby red type lipstick. Those who wear makeup will also often accessorize with horn-rimmed glasses. They may also have their tongue pierced or a small diamond nose piercing, usually preferring to stick with the more subtle and classy piercing. Those who reject makeup are of a slightly different kind and don't accessorize their faces much except for a well-placed eyebrow or lip ring. However, some of the more *extreme* non-makeup Rock Chicks will go overboard with their facial piercings to make up for their lack of makeup. Both types prefer black finger nail polish.

In addition to the head and facial adornments of The Rock Chick, her clothing is often of the thrift store variety. She enjoys finding the Dukes of Hazzard t-shirt or whimsical plaid pants (if plaid pants can ever be considered whimsical) at the local Salvation Army or Goodwill store. Army Surplus stores are always a plus because it is there that she can always locate a good, old pair of army pants and that trucker cap that says "Old Fart" on it. She appreciates the irony of such a cap. If she's lucky, she may also find a smashing chain-wallet to accessorize with. As a rule, The Rock Chick wears t-shirts and hooded, zip-up sweatshirts. She has disdain for shirts that button, unless the buttons are pearl and come on a classic, embroidered cowboy shirt from a local vintage clothing store. She likes to shop these stores as well. She dresses herself in cast-off clothing to make the point that she is opposed to current, high-dollar fashion trends and she strives to assert herself as the essence of antiestablishment. Anything corporate or smelling of mass appeal is offensive to her. She does not wear Diesel, Prada, or Marc Jacobs, and if it's sunny outside, she will wear a cheap pair of aviator sunglasses (circa late '80s Top Gun era) to guard her eyes and make her more mysterious.

But we haven't yet discussed the meaning of her title . . . The Rock Chick. The primary thing about The Rock Chick is her undying loyalty, admiration, and allegiance to her favorite musical bands. Her identity is found in the bands she most adores. These are not bands like The Dave Matthews Band, Third Day, or Matchbox Twenty. For The Rock Chick, the more obscure the band/music, the better, and it is a badge of honor if she is into a group that almost no one has heard of before. She adorns her car with their stickers. (Her car, by the way is usually a lower-priced American-made car that her dad passed down to her, like an early 90s Geo Metro.) The Rock Chick is generally into indie rock bands, emo bands, and the occasional retro music like the Beatles or Frank Sinatra. Rock-a-billy, streetpunk, skatepunk, hardcore, and occasionally, British hip-hop music, find their way into her stereo. She will show her favorite bands her undying loyalty by attending every show within a three-hour drive and by buying every record they release, including imports. Her dedication to them will not falter unless their music video happens to find its way onto MTV or MTV2, at which point she will sell all their records and declare them as having "sold out." This is simply unacceptable to The Rock Chick (because now *everyone* knows about them).

One of The Rock Chick's favorite past-times, besides going to shows, is hanging out in her room listening to music and updating her blog. If she's not there updating her blog and chilling out while listening to music, you can probably bet that she is somewhere *else* with headphones on, listening to music. If she's not listening to music, you may find her at the local independent movie theater watching a Sundance film festival winner or a bad "B movie" (for the irony).

The Rock Chick is also into photography. She doesn't really enjoy *looking* at photography as much as she enjoys *taking* photos. Now she doesn't take pictures of friends or family, like others do, to capture a memory or to remember a special moment in time. She will have none of that because *this* is her primary art form and creative expression and not some cheesy memory to paste in a scrapbook. That's not what photography is for. She uses black and white film only because color is just too typical. She loves taking pictures of inanimate objects, careful to find a unique point of view that no one has ever seen before. Her photos are often fuzzy and abstract—just like the music she likes, but she is bound and determined to express herself through this medium. If she does take a photo of a person, you can bet that they will be out of focus and half out of the frame. The Rock Chick also likes to read. J.D. Salinger, Kurt Vonnegut, Franz Kafka, Allen Ginsberg, and Flannery O'Connor are her favorite authors, and she carries their books in her satchel in hopes that some like-minded soul will spot one of them and strike up a meaningful conversation about the human condition. She doesn't really understand *everything* that her favorite authors write, but she likes to pretend that she does.

As far as school is concerned, she could care less about most classes except for English Lit and Art. Those are the two subjects that she finds fascinating. The rest of school is boring and most of the rest of her classmates are, too. She suffers through and she's not really that happy about it. She is a C- student and manages to get by with just a minimal amount of effort and work because school just really isn't her "thing." Music is her "thing" and while class is in session, she dreams about someday marrying a boy in a band. This is her favorite daydream.

If you haven't figured it out by now, The Rock Chick is a fairly moody girl. She tends to have a chip on her shoulder and gets annoyed easily. She is tragic. She likes to be perceived as tough and unapproachable to outsiders but will cry around other Rock Chicks when she hears a particularly emotional and honest song. Emo music gets her every time. Animals are her soft spot. She loves animals and hates to see one suffer. Even the occasional road kill brings a lump to her throat. Someday, if her dream of marrying a musician doesn't work out, she would be quite happy to become a veterinarian. Or maybe a vegetarian.

Even though The Rock Chick appears to be a loner, she isn't. She does like to spend time to herself, doing her hair and nails (black), but she also socializes with other Rock Chicks and especially boys who are musicians. If there are no musician boys to hang out with at lunch (and by musicians, we don't mean a trombone player in the marching band), she will hang out with other Rock Chicks and mutter sarcastic remarks about the trendy people. The Rock Chick uses sarcasm, irony, and negativity as her shield to keep others at arm's length. There are certain times when she doesn't use sarcasm and will speak honestly from her heart. When this happens, she is usually speaking out about injustices in the world and issues like free speech or the significance of being anti-corporate. But in general politics bore her, and she figures that they are someone else's problem.

You may have noticed that The Rock Chick doesn't have much tolerance for things she doesn't personally enjoy (though she likes to slam those she finds intolerant). She also prides herself on being antiestablishment and a bit on the rebellious, counter-culture side of things. Because of these general tendencies, there are two distinct types of Rock Chicks at church. The first is The Rock Chick who is dragged to church by her family. She really doesn't want to be there because it just isn't her scene, and she thinks that the other kids in the youth group are squares. Because of her love of music, and the church's traditional brand of worship, she may find the whole experience to be something out of a *Leave It To Beaver* episode. Stoic, dry, and stale. Even when churches try to put together a modern worship service for the "young people," she thinks the worship team/band is trying too hard and comes off like posers. This type of Rock Chick, even though she may be a Christian, generally doesn't enjoy going to church. The other type of Rock Chick *loves* going to church and realizes that she is dedicated to following Jesus, who was the greatest rebel and counter-cultural figure of all time. This Rock Chick appropriately sees her own faith and Christianity as an integral part of her identity and the main part of what makes her a radical, a rebel against the lies of a jaded and unbelieving world.

5 Clues that You Might Be the Rock Chick:

1. You have drumsticks in your backpack and you don't play the drums.
2. Your locker, notebooks, textbooks, and bumper of car are wrapped in band stickers
3. You are never without black eyeliner.
4. You save money all year for a trip to Cornerstone, Tom Fest, or the Vans Warped Tour.
5. You never carry a purse, but opt for a chain wallet and a studded belt instead.

WHAT WOULD YOU FIND IN HER LOCKER?
Vinyl records, photographs taken at last summer's indie punk fest

FAVORITE MOVIES: *High Fidelity, Spinal Tap, That Thing You Do* (a guilty pleasure)

FAVORITE MUSIC: Who are we kidding? Relient K, of course. Oh, and anything else anti-corporate like, maybe, Julianna Theory, Bright Eyes, Mineral, or The Promise Ring. The more obscure, the better.

TV CHANNEL OR SHOW: TV is for mindless noncreative androids with no soul.

FAVORITE DRINK: Jones, Barq's Root Beer

SHOES: Chuck Taylors

WEBSITE: www.makeoutclub.com

AFTER SCHOOL JOB: Indie record store, veterinarian's assistant

MAKEUP: Black eyeliner

DID YOU KNOW . . . ? The Rock Chick's Bible cover is made out of shiny duct tape.

THE DiVa

This girl has always existed, though you might not have known too much about her until recently. Over the last few years, a new phenomenon has developed, a "craze," if you will. And through this craze, a distinctive type of girl has emerged and been thrust into spotlight for all the world to see, thanks to a little help from the massively popular TV show *American Idol*. These are the girls who sass back to Simon—you know the ones. We shall bestow upon her the title of The Diva.

You know her by the gleam in her eye and the sly smile across her face. She is ready for the world and is sure that the world is ready for her. But if you think that Divas are only singers with names like Britney, Christina, Jessica, Mandy, and now Kelly or Fantasia, you may need to think again. Not all Divas can sing (as witnessed by some performances on *American Idol*) but all Divas do have several things in common. First of all, The Diva is confident. Supremely confident. Wildly confident, even. She is positive and certain that she is the coolest, the smartest, or the most talented girl around. Sometimes, usually, all three. She may tell you this out loud or she may keep it to herself, but in either case, you can tell. You can always tell. The Diva believes that she has something to offer the world that is undeniable and indispensable, no matter what that "thing" is. It may be singing, it could be theater, or maybe even being a super model. But in every case, her contribution to the world is certainly a public one.

The Diva thrives on being the center of attention because the center of attention is the place to be. And The Diva knows about all the cool places. Being able to capture and hold the attention of others becomes The Diva's full time job. Being the center of attention isn't easy because The Diva must always work to capture and hold other people's attention. She talks just a little bit louder than everyone else at the lunch table, she must be a little bit funnier than other people, she must dress a little more interestingly than other people, and she must have herself more together than other people. She likes it when people talk to her, but she likes it even more when people hear her talk. She doesn't even mind if people talk about her behind her back, because if they do, they are certainly saying how wonderful The Diva is. In situations when nobody is supposed to be talking, like in study hall or the library, The Diva enjoys it if people are simply looking at her. If this happens, The Diva is doing her job. The Diva may even feel led to try out for beauty pageants, because she knows that she's the prettiest girl around.

At her worst, The Diva can be bossy and self-centered, but that is usually when others aren't paying enough attention. She will tend to take social control by force. However, she can be thoroughly charming and at ease when all eyes and ears are turned her way. The Diva appears to be popular but not necessarily well liked. This is something that haunts The Diva, though she chooses not to think much about it. She doesn't spend much time on her faults at all. Now other people's faults are her specialty, and she loves to sit around with a critical eye and discuss them with anyone who will listen. She makes sure to surround herself by people who are a tiny bit beneath her. She could never be upstaged by someone in her own group for that would be disastrous.

Above all, The Diva is a groomer. Grooming is her most time consuming activity, paying particular attention to her hair and face. This is her forward feature to the world, and she is sure to maintain the look of her hair and face at all times. You will find her in the girls' restroom between every class, and she's not necessarily there for the obvious reasons. She camps out in the restroom because of the abundance of large mirrors most useful for her grooming activities. Now we only know this information because we've been told. None of us have ever been inside a girls' restroom to witness this grooming phenomenon, but like we said, we've been told. (We've also heard that girls' restrooms are much nicer than boys'. Why is that? Another subject for another time, we suppose.)

But back on the subject of time . . . grooming time, that is . . . we have done some initial calculations to support our thesis that Divas spend the bulk of their time grooming. After a Diva awakes in the morning, she heads directly for (surprise!) the bathroom, where she showers, does up her hair, and puts on her face. (You didn't know that Divas don't have a face at night, did you? Neither did we.) This morning prep time clocks in at an amazing 1 hour and 45 minutes. To give you an idea of how entirely different this is from a guy's morning, here is a guy's schedule: 2.5 minutes in the shower, 15 seconds of towel

Famous Divas:

J. Lo
Jessica Simpson
Paris Hilton
Oprah Winfrey
Beyoncé

time, 45 seconds to get dressed, 10 seconds to find the ball cap under his bed, and another 2 seconds to apply it to his head in a jaunty manner. If he chooses to brush his teeth (and he may not), add another 45 seconds. This male morning prep time comes to a whopping total of 4.45 minutes. To put it another way, by the time a Diva is lost in the vicious cycle of rinsing and repeating with hair conditioner, the guy is already in his car, backing down the driveway with the stereo blaring.

When The Diva finally arrives at school about 10 minutes after the tardy bell has rung, she does not proceed directly to homeroom, but to the restroom for last minute touch-ups before she faces her public. Add five minutes. Then her daily cycle begins: first period class, restroom, locker, second period class, restroom, locker, third period class . . . you get the picture. By the time that the Diva leaves school at the end of the day, she has added another 45 minutes to her growing grooming total. There is more re-grooming to be done before her after school job or hanging out with friends (add 20 minutes) and then finally before bed at night, The Diva must shred the last vestiges of her face. This painful process takes 35 minutes. If you are still reading and care to know, The Diva has spent a blinding 3 hours and 15 minutes of total daily grooming. Other than sleep, there is no other activity that a Diva does that takes anywhere near that amount of time.

> ## THE DIVA IN 5 WORDS OR LESS:
>
> well-groomed
> trendy
> self-assured
> outgoing
> particular

Since so much of The Diva's time is spent with her outward prep work, you can pretty much count on the fact that she will be late to everything. She is always late, but fashionably so. She has learned long ago that to get away with her lateness, she must turn on her charm so that others won't mind. She's so charming that the teachers don't seem to mind. If she makes her friends late to the movies, she tells them how fabulous they all look and marvels at how much time they must have spent getting ready to go out. This tends to lighten the mood and she's off the hook.

The Diva is undeniably well dressed and must maintain a cutting-edge fashion sense at all times. After all, since she is always in the spotlight, other people look to her to find out the latest style or trend. To maintain this advanced fashion sense, The Diva is dedicated to studying the celebrity scene. She loves to watch award shows like the Oscars, the Grammys, and the American Music Awards. She has numerous subscriptions to magazines such as *Cosmo Girl, Seventeen, Teen People, Jane,* and *US Weekly,* where she is able to track what the stars are doing and wearing. It is here that she learns of the latest fashion tips. She has discovered that she can remain relatively safe from fashion error if she shops at Urban Outfitters.

The Diva's trendy hair color doesn't come in a box, oh, no, it doesn't. Her highlights and lowlights are always done professionally, and never at a sleep over with friends (unlike The Rock Chick). Crest whitening strips, skin care products, hair care products, waxing products, an entire tackle box full of nail care products, pumice stones, loofahs, skin-firming lotion, shimmer lotion, lotion with aloe, and ten different scents of lotion are all necessities and are found to crowd the sink in her bathroom.

It is true that The Diva appears to be quite shallow and is concerned with her looks and social standing. But when she's alone in her room at night, The Diva is a normal girl with all the same cares and concerns that the rest of the girls face. In public, she prefers not to let people see any weaknesses, but in reality The Diva wants to be liked, though she may have a strange way of showing it. And, yes, The Diva is prone to self-absorption, but she also has many good traits. She's positive, confident (yes, that can be a good thing), and has a big heart. And although she's outgoing and never meets a stranger, she probably only has a small group of close friends and she's fiercely loyal to them.

The Diva has a lot in common with The Rock Chick when it comes to church. She puts off the vibe that she doesn't really want to be there though, secretly, she's glad to be there. Sometimes, she's really glad to be there at church, but only if she's asked to speak publicly or sing. If all eyes are on The Diva, then you'll know without a doubt that she's glad to be there. And even though she's always well dressed and perfectly groomed, which can be intimidating, somehow she seems to be a person that brings people together. Maybe that's just because she has the whole youth group's attention.

5 CLUES THAT YOU MIGHT BE THE DIVA

1. You've tried out for *American Idol* every single year. Even though they didn't pick you, you think Paula Abdul is the smartest woman you've ever met.

2. You inadvertently yelp or drop something every time you're not the center of attention. You don't mean to though.

3. You believe your face looks better "in the right light" (stage lights, of course).

4. You talk often about your "big break," and you're not referring to your last boyfriend.

5. Ironically, your name is also Jessica Simpson.

The Homecoming Queen

Next we will start on one of the rarest and yet most obvious types of girl there is, The Homecoming Queen. Don't be misled though: The Homecoming Queen may not always be the actual, elected Homecoming Queen, though she is almost always the most likely candidate, as we shall soon see.

You will only find one or two Homecoming Queens in any school or social setting. The reason for her being both rare and obvious is that she has risen through the ranks of the ordinary, the normal, and the average to the top . . . the very pinnacle of her societal order. She's pretty and she's popular. And there is good enough reason for her meteoric rise in illustriousness.

To start, let's look at the way she might enter a room. If she were to walk in your room at this very instant, she wouldn't explode through the door like The Diva. Neither would she clump into your room like The Rock Chick. She also wouldn't stumble in and trip over her own feet like The Airhead. No, instead, she breezes into a room lightly, as if walking on piles and piles cotton balls or has helium balloons tied to her feet. Either way. Her hair is usually blown back ever so slightly as if there were a small fan pointed at her face. You might even perceive a faint halo/glow about her head and arms. Her smile and teeth would shine up your room like a light, and she might even give you a hug. She is a lot like someone you would see in the movies. She is sweet and ever so classssy. But that is only how she enters a room and doesn't necessarily explain her electric popularity.

The Homecoming Queen's popularity usually begins at home, where she is well liked by her family. Well, actually most girls are well liked by their families. And so is The Homecoming Queen. Her family likes her because they have to (she *is* family after all), but they also like her because she is thoughtful and sweet and looks out for others. She likes to serve around the house by doing dishes, vacuuming the living room, or emptying the trash. She even whistles while she works. This creates a nice atmosphere and kind of lifts the spirit. The Homecoming Queen likes to lift the spirits of others, too. At school she is the champion for the underdog. She hates to see anyone lose or get picked on. If that happens, she is usually right there to offer a kind and encouraging word. Generally speaking, she is kind to everyone she meets. She is positive, outgoing, and has a generally sunny disposition.

Because of her outgoing and sunny personality, The Homecoming Queen enjoys being outdoors and active. She likes to go to school sporting events, especially football, soccer, and baseball because they are outdoor sports and she can be there to cheer her friends on. Cheering is a big thing for The Homecoming Queen. Though this seems like a logical conclusion, a lot of Homecoming Queens are cheerleaders. They really are. It is one of those natural things that she enjoys doing. She just about can't help herself. Seeing others win gives her great satisfaction. She does enjoy the sports, but mainly enjoys the cheering factor. She does not ever participate in organized sports, she just watches from the sidelines and cheers. Hooray!

Since she loves to share her enthusiasm with as many people as possible, she often finds herself in front of a crowd doing things like cheerleading or giving a speech. But being in front of a crowd can be scary or frightening. In order to be comfortable in front of a crowd, it takes one of two things: either you must be confident, or you just don't know any better. For us, when we get on stage, it's usually because we don't know any better . . . any better way to *rock* you, that is. For The Homecoming Queen in front of a crowd, she is confident, and that is one of the keys to her success. And because she is in front of people, most people seem to know who she is. She's unflappable and unwavering in bringing joy and happiness to others. Anyone who can brighten up a room, give a speech or dance, flip and cheer their little hearts out will often become well liked and admired by a large majority of people. This is true of The Homecoming Queen and is the main reason for her popularity.

But before you begin to think that her life is a fairy tale or a classic Cinderella story, we must inform you that The Homecoming Queen does have two evil stepsisters that torment her quite a lot. Well, they really aren't evil, but let's just say that they are girls who don't share The Homecoming Queen's outlook on life. The Poet and The Rock Chick have a hard time accepting any notion of popularity and don't take kindly to her status. They may make snide remarks and talk about her behind her back or they might, in a more drastic instance, try to stick gum in her hair to be mean and funny. This is a bad idea for The Rock Chick and The Poet because though The Homecoming Queen is a kind and friendly sort, she does not have perfect self-restraint; she is an experienced high kicker (cheerleading) and may choose to plant her foot in the throat of any gum-hair sticker. Besides, is that any way for ladies to act? No. It is not. So ladies, keep your gum in your mouths and your feet on the floor.

So we've learned that some people are bitter because of The Homecoming Queen's popularity, but these bitter people are usually never popular. Contrary to common thought, The Homecoming Queen does not always wish herself to be the most popular person around but finds herself well liked because of her winning personality and positive outlook on life. She doesn't determine her own popularity—nobody can do that . . . but others do that for her. Sometimes all the attention she receives embarrasses her, but like anyone, she learns to enjoy it. What she doesn't enjoy, however, is being sad. Being sad or outwardly troubled is a no-no for The Homecoming Queen. She must maintain her composure at all costs. After all, she knows that her countenance can light up a room, and she doesn't want for anyone to be left in the dark, so, even if she's down or troubled, The Homecoming Queen musters up a smile and attempts to move on with life.

For someone who seems a bit out in front of the crowd, you may be surprised to notice that The Homecoming Queen dresses just like the rest of the crowd. Her mode of attire is always fashionable, but she doesn't make too much of it. Whether she shops at the Gap, Abercrombie, or Express, she will always be in step with the current fashion trend . . . though she will lean toward the conservative end of any trend. The Homecoming Queen does not make fashion blunders by wearing anything "edgy" but feels comfortable to fit in with the majority of what's going on fashion-wise or otherwise. The same can be said for her use of makeup or jewelry. If she chooses to wear either, it is done appropriately and with taste.

Here are a few other things to keep in mind to help you spot The Homecoming Queen. Most HQ's, as you might guess, have blonde hair, whether it's natural or not. This doesn't mean that they are an airhead (though they can be); it just means they're blonde. Brown and black-haired girls can also be HQs, though the likelihood of this occurring drops dramatically, respectively speaking. If we were to take an educated guess, it would break out like this: Blonde HQ = 60%, Brunette HQ = 35%, Black haired HQ = 5%. Blondes would definitely win out with an almost 2-to-1 margin. Statistically speaking, redheads are never ever HQs, or at least we've yet to meet one.

It may have been confusing to some for us to refer to a girl as a Homecoming Queen when she isn't necessarily elected Homecoming Queen. This may have led to a state of delirium, dilemma, or delusion. If that is the case, we are sorry and beg your forgiveness. But it is really quite clear, right? Homecoming Queen = nice and popular. Nice and popular = Homecoming Queen. You may also be wondering if this particular girl is ever actually elected as a literal Homecoming Queen at her school. She usually is. The Homecoming Queen has an 85 percent likelihood of being elected as Homecoming Queen. She has a 100 percent chance of being elected to the Homecoming Court (or whatever you call it), which we like to think of as all the runners up. The almost queens.

If you think that The Homecoming Queen appears to have a carefree and charmed life, you might be interested to know that all is not always well in The Homecoming Queen's world. Though well known and admired around school or the town, The Homecoming Queen secretly finds it hard to maintain her "perfect" image. There is a lot of pressure on her to do the right thing and to be the right things always when so many eyes are always on her. She handles the pressure well, but may eventually crack or have to vent to a few close friends in private. She may even feel guilty that she isn't always perfect (as everyone assumes she is).

At church, The Homecoming Queen is the girl that all other girls' mothers wish their daughters would become. She is usually a leader in the youth group and always volunteers for service projects, like helping out at homeless shelters and serving food during a church potluck. She is a highly recognized fixture at all church events. The Homecoming Queen is also a much requested person to do the offertory or "special music," not because she is such a good singer but because people like her.

5 CLUES THAT YOU MAY BE AN HQ:

1. You have no known enemies.
2. Your hairstyle hasn't changed in years—long hair with big loopy curls. Kind of what you'd see at a Miss America pageant. It always looks freshly styled.
3. You never bash on anyone.
4. Your friend's parents never worry about their daughter when she's with you.
5. You have held any or all of these elected titles: Cutest, Most Beautiful, Miss Congeniality, Class Favorite.

WHAT WOULD YOU FIND IN HER LOCKER?
Snapshots of friends, pom poms, Crest whitening strips

EMAIL SIGNATURE OR QUOTE WOULD BE: "Smile, God loves you!"

FAVORITE MOVIES: *Never Been Kissed, While You Were Sleeping, The Princess Diaries*

FAVORITE MUSIC: John Mayer

AFTER SCHOOL JOB: Babysitter, Candy striper

CAR: Jetta, VW bug

EXTRA CURRICULAR ACTIVITIES: cheerleading

POST COLLEGE OCCUPATION: News Anchor, Weather Person on local news, Public Relations

MAKEUP: Bonnie Bell, Cover Girl

Brian Pittman on
THE HOMECOMING QUEEN:

In junior high, I started to notice the girlies. I like 'em. I was looking back through some old year books and realized it is so crazy how much we all change from junior high to high school and the years after. I know every school has one girl that just really stands out . . . the babeasauraus. In my school, there was this girl named Tracy who always had the best of everything. Every year she always won Best Dressed, Nicest Smile, Best Hair. Blah blah blah. (Maybe I am bitter b/c I thought I had better hair than her. You didn't hear that from me.) When it came to school dances or homecomings, she always seemed to be in the spotlight. I remember seeing her at a football game in her dress and she seemed to be glowing. You could tell she put a lot of work into how she presented herself, and it always seemed to work for her.

Tracy always had a smile and seemed to be pretty genuine with everyone around her. We were in gym class and once or twice a year, we would have to do the whole coed thing. We were bowling that semester, and it came time to match up with your partner. The teachers were together pairing people up and, sure enough, Tracy and I were put together. Every guy in class let me know how much they wanted to be me. I got to know her a little in between talking strikes and 7-10 splits. She seemed to break the stereotype of a snob and being too wrapped up in herself. Oh, but no, I wasn't interested in her. I am a rocker and her fave band was Dave Matthews. . . .

THE MATHLETE

Hers is a strange yet beautiful world—a foreign land whose stamp is not found in our passports. The Mathlete lives in a world of equations, theorems, and proofs—a world where the quadratic formula can lead to the answers for her life's many questions. Words like polynomial, coefficient, cosine, and Pythagorean theorem hold great meaning for her, and even as she sleeps these words float through her head like dandelion fuzz on a breezy summer day.

Like any good Athlete, The Mathlete is an intimidator. A quiet intimidator. She intimidates, not by her physical brawn or athletic skill but by the sharp gleam in her eye as she grips her number 2 pencil and scribbles down answers to questions that the rest of us would never think to ask. The Mathlete walks with a permanent slump that has been caused by the excessive trauma of her overloaded backpack. If The Mathlete's mother knows how to sew, she has likely had to re-sew the straps back on her daughter's backpack several times due to the excessive weight load of books she always carries with her. Hers is a burden that she carries with dignity and a slight limp.

The Mathlete is smart and others know it. But don't let her title fool you. There is a lot more going on in her head than just numbers and equations. The Mathlete's field of expertise is always math, but she also may expand her brain's capacity to include history, geography, astronomy, biology, and chemistry. Though she is a fine reader, she does not usually do quite as well in English or literature because it all seems just a little too easy for her. Don't worry though, she is able to maintain her status as a straight A student.

Like the regular Athlete, Mathletes are a competitive bunch, but you won't find them all riled up for an intramural basketball game after school. This competitor's field of battle lies in the classroom, on tests. She competes not only against herself in trying the make the perfect grade on these so-called tests, but she also contends against her classmates, though they may not know it. She loves to compare grades, casually asking her neighbors what they got on *their* test, or slyly glancing over at their desks while she leans down to pick up a fresh pencil out of her backpack. When she finds out that she scored a higher grade than her neighbor, she quietly sits back in her chair with an unmistakable air of triumph. Her victories are small and may go unnoticed by the majority, but come graduation time when the Valedictorian steps up to the podium to give her closing speech, you recognize her and realize that her transformation is now complete. The Mathlete has become the Valedictorian. Or Salutatorian . . . or whatever. But before her meteoric rise to the starry heights of Valedictorian-infused intellectual success, she labors in relative obscurity, competing on tests and homework assignments, and studying hard for her big, somewhat public competition.

What is The Mathlete's big competition you might ask? Well, we are here to tell you all about that. With names like "MathCounts," "Future Problem Solvers" (FPS), "American Math Competition"

(AMC), "American Invitational Math Exam" (AIME), and the grand-daddy of them all, the "United States of America Mathematical Olympiad" (USAMO), Mathletes are able to break out of their comfort zones and test their enormous cranial capacities against others with equally colossal brains from other schools, towns, and even other states in all sorts of Math Matches. These competitions may involve simply sitting in a room at a host site (possibly a local university auditorium or a classroom from a rival high school) and taking a test. The fancier competitions, however, have the look and feel of a poor man's game show on television. Sitting on stage in metal chairs behind a folding table draped in a black cloth, the competing Mathletes' hands hover over buzzers as the moderator throws out questions to be answered aloud by the quickest contestant. Unlike a game show on TV, where the quickest buzzer hand and the answer may win you a new car or a trip to Hawaii, the winner only receives a ribbon and a pat on the back. This may seem anticlimactic to some but can easily rank as one of The Mathlete's proudest moments. Those who don't win the Math Matches are sad and dejected but determined to go home, study their brains out, and maybe even practice their quick-draw, buzzer-smacking skills. Like any competitor, The Mathlete knows the thrill of victory and the bitter, crushing disappointment of defeat.

Though Mathletes will receive little glory upon their return to school, they will be rewarded with a trip to McDonalds before they begin the drive back home, during which the contestants can commiserate or celebrate, depending on the outcome of the competition. A glimpse into the conversations of these Mathletes on these occasions proves that their world is indeed a strange and mysterious one. Because, it is one thing to "do" math and write it down for a test, and it is quite another to sit around and voluntarily talk about it while you knock back a quarter-pounder and fries. Amongst the comparing of answers, it would not be uncommon to hear The Mathlete regale her comrades with a tale of how she could not believe that when she got to that question about the parabola, she totally forgot the formula to find the axis of symmetry. She tells them that, fortunately, at the last minute she remembered: y equals ax-squared minus bx plus c, and was able to finish the problem. At this moment, her friends will all simultaneously open their mouths to say, "But . . . ," at which point our Mathlete will interrupt and say, "I know, can you believe it? It wasn't until after I turned in my answer sheet that I realized it's: y equals ax-squared *plus* bx plus c." Her fellow Mathletes will let out sympathetic "ahhhs," and continue telling their own tales of "silly" mistakes and "easy" questions that got away.

The Mathlete is a quiet sort with a distinct air of superiority. She knows better than to talk too much and is typically a good listener. You may get the picture that The Mathlete is not a very social person, outside of study groups, because, frankly, she just doesn't seem to have much spare time. In addition to her fellow Mathletes, she counts books among her better friends. The Mathlete may secretly hold some level of embarrassment about her extra-curricular academic activities—for instance, she would not speak about her involvement in Problem Solvers of America to anyone but her fellow Mathletes.

THE MATHLETE IN 5 WORDS OR LESS:

brilliant
studious
competitive
problem-solving
buttoned-up

The Mathlete loves to wear cardigan sweaters. They are her favorite. She also has a closet full of long-sleeved, buttoned-collar Oxford shirts, mainly in the colors of white, light blue, and pink. She will wear the khaki pants and the plaid skirts with certain regularity. Basically, anything that gives off a classic collegiate look is an awesome clothing choice for The Mathlete. Her hair is always in a ponytail. Always. No exceptions. Hair hanging in her face while bent over a study book is unacceptable. Because she only ever gives off the ponytail look, this makes for a nice switch-a-roo when, at an unsuspecting moment, she lets her hair down, shakes it all out, and pulls off her thick coke bottle glasses. Who knew? She was beautiful all this time. This seems to work well in the movies and we like it in real life, too.

One of the things that we really like about this girl is that she is into gadgets, just like boys are, only they're different gadgets. Her primary required gadget is a TI-84 Plus Graphing Calculator, which has more buttons than a waitress's apron at T.G.I. Fridays, and she knows what each button does. She uses this technological wonder to double-check her calculations and equations. The Mathlete may also be fond of a slide rule, a protractor, compasses, and other less interesting items.

A strange phenomenon occurs with a slight majority of Mathletes at some point in their lives. Usually, sometime during elementary school, she finds herself affixed with some sort of metal-bracing device, and whether it's to straighten her teeth or her back, it has the unfortunate habit of needing to be worn in public. This often brings derision or scorn by others. It is our opinion that these metal bracing devices actually accelerate The Mathlete's brain growth, resulting in an unusually higher IQ at an earlier age. Brian thinks that such metal devices might actually act as an antenna where The Mathlete's brain is actually downloading data, formulas, and binary equations from a NASA satellite because *how else* would all that stuff get in her head?

But for all her smarts and brilliance, The Mathlete has a hard time with relationships. To some, she is unapproachable because she is so studious, smart, and out of their league. To others who venture closer, she can be a bit over analytical and "right." She is right most of the time, and at times her "rightness" is a turn-off. Other people know they can be wrong and admit it, but this is hard for her. The Mathlete also appears to be more consumed with finding the answer than just forgetting the question and having a little fun. Frivolity and silliness are sometimes missing from the Mathlete's world.

The Mathlete at church is a bit of a frustration to her youth group leader. She is the person who always asks the questions that are just too hard (or ridiculous) to answer, like "Can God make a rock sooooo big and heavy that He can't lift it?" or technical questions like "So if Noah built and ark that was ___ cubits long, and a cubit equals ___ feet, that would be about the size of a ____. Now how could he fit two of every animal in an ark that small?!" She may also be caught spacing off during a Sunday morning sermon. If she appears to be spacing off, you can bet that she is probably counting the number of wooden planks in the ceiling and seeing if that number is divisible by 3.

5 CLUES THAT YOU MIGHT BE THE MATHLETE

1. Your role models are Pasteur and Einstein.
2. When greeted with the phrase, "Word up," you ask, "Word up, where?"
3. You only write in pencil.
4. You have no framed pictures of friends or horses in your room. Only certificates.
5. Ribbons, ribbons, ribbons.

WHAT WOULD YOU FIND IN HER LOCKER?
Practice buzzer, extra math books, at least 3 different calculators

AWARDS: 1st Grade Spelling Bee Champion, 2nd . . . 3rd . . . 4th . . . blah blah on and on

EMAIL SIGNATURE: "Man is equally incapable of seeing the nothingness from which he emerges and the infinity in which he is engulfed."

Blaise Pascal,
French mathematician,
physicist

FAVORITE MOVIES: *A Beautiful Mind, Spellbound*

FAVORITE MUSIC: Devo, The Proclaimers, They Might Be Giants, Danielson Family

TV CHANNEL OR SHOW: Discovery Channel

WEBSITE: http://www.mensa.org/

PICTURE/POSTERS: periodic table, Einstein

SUMMER JOB: Interns at a local accounting firm

MAKEUP: when she remembers

DID YOU KNOW . . . ? She loves to study and learn—really!!

Matthew Hoopes talks about
THE MATHLETE:

Sonia was one of my good friends throughout my entire school career. Seriously, she was in every class as me all the way to senior year and while we wouldn't even hang out outside of school, she was the kind of girl that you eat lunch with and are just comfortable being around. She is probably one of the smartest people that I have ever come in contact with. I think she goes to Ohio State now and is going to be a doctor of some kind. She was in every advanced class and really set the curve high in all subjects . . . she was ahead of the class in math and also was a very talented and creative writer. Sonia was a teacher's pet, although it seemed like she didn't even try to be . . . she wasn't a suck up, but she was just really into learning. She wore very "normal" clothes and you could tell she was not really into fashion or music, but she always looked presentable and dignified, while being sure not to stick out too much.

I remember the first time in junior high when I saw her in a dress and remember thinking, "Wow, she is really pretty and I never even noticed before." I guess she was more like a sister to me, which is easy when you kind of grow up with someone. She was a very moral girl and she almost reminds me of Lisa Simpson in that she is such a talented do-gooder who takes school more seriously than it has to be. She was never really into the same things as me . . . like sports and music and video games, so maybe that is why we never seemed to have a lot to talk about other than the big test coming up. She was the kind of girl that graduated with like a 4.8 or something and probably didn't have to pay a dime for college. So maybe all that hard work did pay off . . . but sometimes I wonder how she is doing right now. I guess I will have to wait until the class reunion . . . ha.

The Overachiever

Have you ever received your yearbook at the end of the school year and as you were leafing through the pages, you started to suspect there was something strange going on. Page after page revealed the same familiar face smiling broadly in different settings over and over again. It kinda creeps you out a bit. What is going on? Is there some sort of strange, subversive scheme going on here? She grins up at you like she knows something you don't. And she may. She knows how many times her face appears in the yearbook—the exact number. Why? There are two reasons. The first is that she's the yearbook editor and put this thing together in the first place. She has left her mark, by way of photos and memories on her school. Her lineage, her legacy, her picture is there staring at you from page to page in the school yearbook. But the second and more profound reason for her overwhelming yearbook presence is that she is The Overachiever!

Yes, that's right—The Overachiever. Like a hamster on a wheel, like a junkie looking for a fix, this girl keeps on going and going from one activity to the next, never stopping to slow down. She's all motion, except to have her photo taken (presumably for the yearbook). She's a blur of accomplishment. You know her well because you can't escape her. Her accomplishments precede her and that's just the way she likes it. She has managed to become the student body president and the pep-club president at the same time. Besides being the yearbook editor, she has volunteered to coordinate the decorations for all the school dances and works in the school's front office for extra credit. She makes the morning announcements over the PA system during homeroom hour and sometimes introduces the guest speakers during school assemblies. She sings in the choir and is the student assistant to the drama teacher. She is not really into sports but finds time to run track. She's everywhere, all the time, in every way. And that's just at school.

After school The Overachiever volunteers three afternoons a week at the youth center downtown, tutoring and playing with disadvantaged kids. On Saturdays, she hands out magazines and candy at the hospital. She teaches four year olds in Sunday school and helps lead music on Wednesday nights at church. She has also has a summer internship at the local newspaper when she is not life guarding at her neighborhood swimming pool. Unless The Overachiever has unlocked the portal to a world where a single day consists of more than twenty-four hours (which would not be surprising, given her other extraordinary achievements), we believe that she is also . . . very, very tired. Though one might not know that by looking at her. She always appears to have super-human energy. Well, maybe she isn't so tired after all, and it is just that the rest of the world is lazy. Yeah, that's it! It makes us feel better to think of her being the only non-lazy one; otherwise, we would all suck while she would not. This way, we (the lazy) are normal and she is the not normal one.

From what we can gather, the motivation behind the Overachiever's over achieving is one or more of the following things:

Number 1. On the one hand, she may be someone who genuinely

wants to do good in the world and cares about other people. She may have an extreme case of the servant syndrome, sort of like Martha in the Mary/Martha/Jesus story in the Bible.

Number 2. On the other hand, she knows that her college applications are just around the corner, and nothing says, "I belong at Harvard University" like an extra long list of extracurricular activities in addition to her glittering GPA. The Overachiever believes that her "permanent record" will indeed follow her the rest of her life. She carries a copy of her resume in her backpack, just in case. And every morning before school, she goes over her Franklin Covey daytimer to think and plan out her day. Every moment must count. Every grade, every test, every class, every club, every activity. It all counts towards the future and the future must count.

Number 3. The Overachiever may have a wee bit of selfishness involved with her busyness, and it is that she prefers to be the leader. She loves to have people look up to her and for people to think highly of her because of her many, many accomplishments. She loves to be in charge and often doesn't trust others to do things the "right way." Her way is certainly the right way and sometimes it's just easier to do things herself. This works out well for the rest of us, the lazy ones, who prefer a weekend long movie rental marathon instead of raking the leaves at a widowed neighbor's house. It works out well, unless of course, you happen to be the unfortunate person who forgot to bring the green balloons that you were assigned for the school dance that she is organizing. This is the sort of thing that might put The Overachiever over the edge. Then you will be on the receiving end of The Overachiever's wrath. So beware, green balloon person, beware.

The dress code of The Overachiever is fairly predictable and it begins early on. In junior high, The Overachiever will be the one who dresses in collegiate attire, wearing sweatshirts with her favorite university's logo splashed across the front. This is a signal to let others know that she is thinking far ahead of junior high and high school. That she is ready for the big time, real world of college. In high school, she has out-grown her college clothes fascination and instead wears professional-looking clothes, like what she imagines she will wear on her first *real* job interview. High school fashion is not in her repertoire and is only for the small-minded, trendy people who aren't smart enough to be thinking ahead. The only time that The Overachiever dresses the part of the high school student is for pep rallies (she is the pep-club president, remember?) when she will don the school colors and paint the school symbol on her cheek. She doesn't do this begrudgingly, but with the knowledge that school spirit is her *job*. She can put on her business suit attire tomorrow.

The Overachiever may be outgoing or somewhat quiet. You will find Overachievers of both kinds and everything in between. We have seen painfully shy Overachievers or talkative, in-your-face Overachievers. In every case, The Overachiever tries to think and act older than she really is. The greatest compliment someone could pay The Overachiever is that she is "beyond her years." This will make

THE OVERACHIEVER IN 5 WORDS OR LESS:

driven
over-extended
afraid-to-fail
popular
Martha Stewart

her flush with pride. The lazy people tend to think of her as a suck-up. Because of her incessant activity, tightly wound persona, and wannabe-older-than-she-looks condition, The Overachiever often teeters on the edge of many people's tolerance threshold and can unfortunately bring out ill-will among the more common, average, and under achievers.

Because The Overachiever is involved in everything, she knows everyone. She has acquaintances in every social stratum, but her tight schedule doesn't often allow time for casual conversation. If this is the case, some might come to realize that at the end of high school that she doesn't have many (if any) close personal friends. She may have hundreds of acquaintances but might realize a little too late that she has traded relationships for what she thinks is a good-looking resume. She has desired people's admiration and respect for what she has accomplished rather than who she is. She might not even really know who she is apart from the things she does.

Since she's Martha in the Mary/Martha equation in the Bible, this comes out even more so at church. She is a self-appointed leader. She will most likely assume the role of Senior Executive Assistant to the Youth Pastor and be the one to order the pizzas and organize the youth group New Year's Eve sleepover at the church. She may also make photocopies of the Sunday school lessons and arrive early to place them on each person's chair. Sometimes, the Overachiever may also press her case to advance to the "College and Career" Sunday school class because she just can't deal with all the immature high schoolers (she being one herself). The Overachiever also sings in the choir and volunteers to sing the special music regularly. Sometimes, this do-good attitude can result in The Overachiever thinking that she can somehow earn God's favor. She can't, you know.

5 clues that you might be the overacHiever:

1. You are a member of more than six after school activities. This includes sports and after school jobs.
2. You spend between 10:30pm and 1:00am scrapbooking the day's activities.
3. You have been looking into various college programs since junior high.
4. It is assumed you will be the class president—every year.
5. You've checked to see what the minimum age is for applying for *The Apprentice*.

WHAT WOULD YOU FIND IN HER LOCKER?

College applications (and at least two are to Ivy League Schools), inspirational sayings on colored index cards, *7 Habits of Highly Effective Teenagers*

EMAIL SIGNATURE: "Failure is not the only punishment for laziness; there is also the success of others."

Jules Renard (1864–1910)

TV CHANNEL OR SHOW: *The Apprentice*

FAVORITE CELEBRITY: Donald Trump, Reese Witherspoon

FAVORITE DRINK: Red Bull and Diet Coke

MOST FAMOUS OVERACHIEVER: Oprah

WEBSITE: www.youngrepublicans.com or www.yda.org, depending on her preference.

PROBABLE NICKNAMES: Type A

AFTER SCHOOL JOB: Red Cross volunteer, tutoring underprivileged kids

DID YOU KNOW . . . ? The Olsen twins owned their own production company (Dualstar Productions) and were multi-millionaires by the age of six. Now that's what we call Overachievers.

THE POET

t's after school and her long hair is pulled back and held back in a wad by two chopsticks. Sweat drips off her nose in a cloud of steam, and the din of anxious espresso drinkers makes it impossible to think. The tip jar is unusually empty yet the cash register rings with repetitive frequency. Everybody loves a good, local coffee shop, but not everybody makes a second home in one. Except for The Poet.

Full time student and part time barista, The Poet wears long, flowing Bohemian skirts, and a peasant blouse. She wears Birkenstocks every day with every outfit and if it's cold out, she wears colored socks to match her skirt. Her hemp, braided necklace is snug enough to almost choke her, but it never does. Sometimes her hair does get tangled up in it and that is just no good. Only when her hair is down can you appreciate her dedication and patience for her hair-growing abilities. The Poet has hair down to the middle of her back, if not longer. She carries with her two primary items that you rarely spot her without. The first is an army green knapsack filled with books by obscure modern poets and journals filled with her own obscure poetry. She may also have an extra pair of hair sticks, a couple of rubber bands, and a dental hygiene kit complete with toothbrush and Tom's of Maine natural toothpaste as she is constantly warding off coffee-stained teeth.

The other thing she routinely carries with her is her acoustic guitar case, strapped to her back. She doesn't play the guitar all that well, but she is taking lessons from an old hippie who frequents her coffee shop. She just knows that one day her poems will be put to music. Her own music. On her own guitar. She is kind of like Phoebe from *Friends*, hoping someday to play her epic poem/song ("Smelly Cat") during her break at the coffee shop and hear polite applause once she's finished. And hopefully, no one will snicker. . . . She can be found on Saturdays in a park or on a college campus, sitting beneath a giant old oak tree, plucking a note or two and singing out her poem song about the injustice of jilted love.

To get to the park or to school or to her after school job, The Poet drives a twenty-two-year-old Volvo that belches clouds of gray smoke and tells the world exactly what she believes in. She wants Tibet, trade, and the whales all to be free. Mean People Suck and NPR are also proudly promoted via her overcrowded bumper full of stickers. Green Peace and the National Park Service both receive free advertising courtesy of her car. At times when The Poet is convicted about the smog her car regularly emits, she may ride her bicycle instead, which is a beachcomber complete with a wicker basket attached to the front handlebars. On a happy day, she will carry a bunch of fresh cut flowers in her bike basket. She thinks that animals are to be loved, not eaten, which makes her a partial vegetarian. She will eat fish, but only because fish are kind of ugly and don't have feelings. She likes to shop at health food stores and drinks a shot of wheat grass with her smoothie every morning. We are told that she does indeed wash her hair, but leaves it at that. No hair mousse or curling irons for The

Poet. We already know that she has good dental hygiene, but she prefers using rock deodorant and will not shave her legs or under her arms for months on end. This is kinda creepy to us.

When at school, The Poet likes to sit alone at lunch and write poems about the lowly high school people she's forced to coexist with for the time being. She brings her own lunch, as eating in the school cafeteria is surely supporting some corporate monster that she boycotts. Instead, she brings herbal tea and fresh granola with fruit and vanilla yogurt. She may also indulge in a tofu sandwich on wheat bread with sprouts and tomato. The Poet is quite creative at coming up with ingenious excuses to skip gym. She believes that sweating is for the unenlightened, and she has better ways to contribute to the earth. Besides, she hasn't shaved her legs in months and NOBODY wants to see her in gym shorts. It's not that she isn't athletic. She loves playing Frisbee or hackey sack in the park with other Poet girls on the weekend, but the idea of playing dodge ball during sixth period gym class makes her stomach turn.

The Poet is a good student, however, and takes her studies seriously. She isn't involved in many extra-curricular activities, but surprisingly enough, each year she nominates herself to run for student government. It's not that she wants to win a popularity contest, but because she recognizes an inequality that must be addressed, and if she doesn't do it, who will? The Poet's mission is to bring peace and tranquility to her world and those around her but she gets ticked off and upset when no one else seems to care. The Poet is very politically active, both in school and out.

The Poet prefers to date an older "man," so after school she drives her Volvo to the local community college to visit her "college" boyfriend, since all the high school boys are beneath her. High school boys could never understand her poetry anyway. Her soul. Her deep well of feelings and prose. But a community college guy on the other hand . . .

The Poet is also very much into art class. She loves to carry her oversized, black portfolio stuffed with sketches and supplies. Her favorite medium is charcoal and conté crayons because they are messy and she really loves to get *into* her art—especially if she is *wearing* as much art supply as ends up on the paper. After a particularly strenuous art class, you might see her in the halls with black smudges on her forehead and spray adhesive on her hands. She dreams of one day getting a book of her poetry published along with her own illustrations. Maybe when she is older, she will write and illustrate a line of children's books.

Unlike The Rock Chick, The Poet isn't all that tragic, but she *is* dark and philosophical. She thinks that being "dark" is cool and makes her mysterious. Her favorite poet is Sylvia Plath and she lets other know that. Sylvia Plath was certainly dark and that's a cool thing to The Poet, but it's all for show. She does things to get a rise out of others—to see how people respond to her. She holds people out at arm's length until she is sure that they can be trusted. The Poet does have a group of friends that she trusts. They are a lot like her and enjoy many of the same things but on the whole, The Poet is a bit on the introspective side. She enjoys reading, writing, doing her art, or practicing her guitar. Since these are not group activities, she does spend a fair amount of time by herself. This doesn't mean that she's necessarily a loner though.

The Poet is a girl who wishes she were alive in the 60s because if she were, there would surely be more people who "get" her. That was a generation of people whose motto was "Love, Peace, and Flower Power." They were full of idealism, feminism, and all sorts of "isms." The Poet wishes she could have been a part of all that. But then she remembers that her parents were of that generation and they are so square and unhip these days. Uh oh . . . is that going to happen to her? The very thought of it makes The Poet quake in her *knee-high, leather-moccasin, lace-up boots*. It is a thought that she quickly erases from her mind.

Her musical tastes also fall in line with the 60s, and she listens to much vintage music. She loves to listen to old scratchy vinyl records of Janis Joplin, Jimi Hendrix, and The Butterfield Blues Band. But unfortunately, she can't listen to old scratchy vinyl records in her car so she does settle for some more "contemporary" artists who have made music in the CD era. Artists like Phish, Widespread Panic, moe., Dave Matthews, Ani DiFranco, and Maroon 5 suit her just fine. If she's feeling especially spirited and in a bit of a hip-hop mood, Jurassic 5 will do the trick.

The Poet is an idealist and is not always in complete touch with reality. She can tends to prefer her own agenda over that of other people. She may talk of peace while arguing over the subject of war. Kind of like The Mathlete, she prefers to be right instead of taking other people's viewpoints into account.

The Poet's idea of church is sitting in a field reading the King James Version of the Bible—because it's more poetic and reads like Shakespeare. But if she finds herself in a regular church setting, she can bring an emotional, mystical element to church and her youth group. She most likely has really thought about and researched her faith, so that she's very comfortable with what she believes. She's very in touch with her feelings and will be a good listener and sharer for the group, if she is able to suppress her own opinion long enough to allow others to share.

5 CLUeS That YOU MiGHT Be THe POeT:

1. Your backpack has no room for textbooks because it's full of personal poetry journals and dream journals.

2. Your clothes always smell of Nag Champa.

3. You can make a mean soy latte.

4. The idea of living in a commune and growing your own vegetables and stuff appeals to you.

5. You will only use herbal medicines that are not tested on animals of any kind.

WHAT WOULD YOU FIND IN HER LOCKER? Flyers for a poetry reading at the coffee shop where she works, poetry books, art supplies

EMAIL SIGNATURE: "It is more natural to me, lying down.

Then the sky and I are in open conversation,

And I shall be useful when I lie down finally:

Then the trees may touch me for once, and the flowers have time for me."

-Sylvia Plath, "I Am Vertical"

FAVORITE MUSIC: Sarah McLachlan, David Gray, Indigo Girls, may have made a secret Nick Lachey compilation CD that's labeled "English term paper"

TV CHANNEL OR SHOW: Television is for unintelligent mindless androids who enjoy being spoon-fed what the corporate monster wants them to eat.

FAVORITE DRINK: Coffee or herbal tea

SHOES: Birks or none at all

FAVORITE AUTHOR: Wendell Berry

PROBABLE NICKNAMES: Granola

AFTER SCHOOL JOB: Local coffee house that is the opposite of Starbucks

CLOTHING LABEL: Clothes bought in second-hand stores and thrift shops that don't normally have labels

MAKEUP: of course not

DID YOU KNOW . . . ? That the polar icecaps are melting at an alarming rate?

Dr. Dave gets his fiber with granola . . .

"Hang on, check the side of the box. How much fiber is in it?" Ahhhhhhh! I hate that! Who cares! Does it taste good? That's the first question. Well, maybe not the first. There was someone who said, "Moderation in all things," and I agree with him. That is probably one of the wisest things ever uttered by human lips. It's really great if the food is healthy. Really, I like healthy food. But come on, let's just relax a little bit.

My friend Rebekkah met her husband, Kayle, at a rock show. That says a little something about a person, so he figured that they'd have some things in common right away. But it did take him a little extra time to figure out what kind of situation he was getting himself into. I found out that Rebekkah was quite aware of her "healthy lifestyle" obsession. She went on her first date with Kayle and deliberately tricked him into thinking she was "normal." That's right, they went out to dinner and everything was great. However, little did Kayle know that Rebekkah had ordered and eaten French fries for the sole purpose of tricking him. Really, she actually ate fries with this in mind! "I should order fries, . . . yes, that's what I'll do, he won't think I'm weird if I eat fries." Quite a plan, huh? Well, it seemed to have worked. They continued to date, and Rebekkah eased Kayle into accepting the extreme health demands that cause her to be called, "super health girl." And it only follows that Kayle became a full believer and assimilated himself into the order. Now he is "super health guy!"

Matt Hoopes on
THE POET:

I remember the first time I met Sarah, and I can't be for sure, but I think she was wearing a tie-dyed shirt and bell-bottom jeans ... or at least that is how I remember her. You know, it is funny that even as people change and go through different phases and styles, you always kind of associate them with one. And Sarah was about as arty as they come; she was a very free-thinking spirit who made a habit of questioning authority and the truth, fighting social injustices, and making it absolutely clear that she was not on the beaten path of life.

While I never heard her poetry or songs, I am sure that she has written volumes. I remember the first time I talked to her and it seems like almost every conversation I had with her somehow turned to music. But anyway, when we would talk about music, I remember repeatedly talking to her about how I didn't like a certain album as much because the production was so bad, and she would get mad and say that I should listen to the song and let it speak to me rather than try to analyze everything. She said that maybe because I was in a band and played guitar, that I over analyze the technical aspects of music, such as chord structure, guitar tones, and melody lines rather than the song as a whole or, more importantly, what it is about. While we had our differences about what music we liked, we actually probably had more similarities. We were both really into a lot of the same bands, and I would see her at shows a lot around our town and that is usually where I would talk to her, unless I ran into her at Borders or Starbucks.

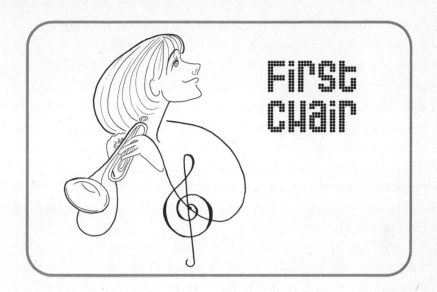

First Chair

n life, there are two types of busses that most folks hope they never have to ride. First, there's the short bus and then comes the band bus. The band bus is where you'll find our next variety of girl . . . a girl that's near and dear to our hearts. Here she comes now, down the hall, walking slowly and clutching a small black box/case by its handle. She walks with her shoulders slumped forward ever so slightly and her eyes are mostly on the ground. You've seen her a hundred times before and you might not know her name, yet chances are, she knows yours. At first glance you might think this girl to be sad, but she isn't. What you are witnessing is only the civilian side of this definitive two-sided girl. There is another completely different side to this girl that you will only see if you too find yourself standing at attention in perfect formation on the practice football field at 6:30 a.m., *in the morning*. She might not fit with the "in" crowd, but in the band room, the band bus, or the football field at halftime, she's a star! Ladies and Gents, we present to you . . . First Chair.

While the rest of the world and their friends are chatting it up at the concession stand during half-time at the football game, there she is, on the field, dressed in the most unfortunate outfit and playing her heart out on that squeaky clarinet for the enjoyment of anyone who will listen. With a plume of feathers sprouting from her cap, she holds her head high and marches side-by-side, step-by-step, to the beat of a different drummer. It is a strange alternate universe in which she lives . . . a society and world unto itself where noisy, prank-filled bus trips are the norm, and spit valves are released with regularity. An outsider will never understand the strong, compelling force that is The Band.

First Chair is one of the most misunderstood girls there is. The reason that the world doesn't understand First Chair is that they have never been in band and have never been in her shoes. And not that they'd want to, because she is forced to wear the goofiest looking shoes ever made, called Dinkles (http://www.dinkles.com). These are standard issue for every marching band girl (or boy)—a must have for the clarinet carrying, marching in time, musical mistress. No, she doesn't wear them around except for marching band, but shoes are beside the point, really. The reason she is misunderstood is because of her unusual passion and drive to make music with others. First Chair loves the band and the band is like a family to her. The skill, talent, and coordination it takes to make music with other people is like a beautiful and complicated dance . . . a dance among friends. And it's also like a team sport. To perform and execute a complicated piece of music (like "Louie, Louie" or "Oye Como Va") while marching around in silly uniforms is very much like a basketball team winning the state championship. There's teamwork, grace, and skill involved in either, and there is much satisfaction to be found in such activities.

But for whatever reason, band people tend to get picked on a lot, especially First Chair. Maybe it's because of the uniforms, because of the un-cool music, or because of the public spectacle involved that many outsiders like to ridicule First Chair. "Dork," "Geek," and "Nerd" are often adjectives that are used as insults directed toward First Chair. Though this is quite common, it is not something we endorse or find particularly funny. What we do find amusing, however, is that those very insults that are meant to hurt her feelings are often times the very thing that makes her strong, confident, and secure with herself. Once First Chair realizes that she is different than all the non-band people and, even though they might find her "band-ness" strange, she realizes that she is not alone. There are others just like her who share her love of marching around and making music. Everybody wants to be understood, and she soon realizes that she is understood and known by other First Chairs. They become like a second family to her. She begins to love the fact that she's different, proud of it, in fact. There is strength in numbers, and the band provides her a sense of place and order in an otherwise messy world.

First Chair lives, thrives, and survives within the circle of the band. But take her outside of band and put her in, say, Home Economics class, and she is lost. She is in a foreign land. She becomes quiet and reserved and tends to keep to herself. She shies away from unwanted attention and likes to hang out on the periphery and watch from a distance. In social situations, she is guarded, and rightly so. Without the protection and comfort of the band, she is wary of being recognized, made fun of, or ridiculed. But whether she feels vulnerable or not, she is quietly confident of who she is. In public, she is a spectator, an observer, a wallflower. That is, unless there are fellow First Chairs around. In this case, she will tend to huddle with them and you will see her come out of her shell a little bit.

There are three social situations where you can witness the First Chair come out of her shell and not be afraid to be herself: The first and most obvious is in the band room, where she is totally free to laugh, cry, and toot her own horn, so to speak. The next is the band bus, where all manner of tomfoolery and nonsense occurs. (The First Chair is usually the ringleader and life of the party on the band bus.) And lastly, the First Chair is at home in church. At church she feels safe and is able to be herself. If you haven't had a chance to see the band girl in any of these settings, you might have no real idea who the First Chair really is.

If you are out on the town, you will have the hardest time trying to spot the First Chair because she appears very normal looking. The First Chair dresses in a conservative, ordinary way. She shops most frequently at Target and Old Navy so that she is not wearing anything too crazy or too flashy. She does not like drawing attention to herself outside of The Band. Her hair is shoulder length and naturally colored.

First Chair in 5 Words or Less:

dedicated
talented
sincere
focused
a performer

First Chair girls do not find reason to spend a lot of extra time at a beauty salon getting their hair and nails done. This is for the more trendy girls and besides, who in their right mind would spend a lot on money on their hair and nails when you know that you will have to crush a marching band hat on your head or risk mangling your nails in the keys of your clarinet. Not the First Chair, that's for sure. Some First Chairs do wear makeup, but some do not. That is left up to the individual. As a rule, the First Chair prefers to fit in and go with the flow.

First Chair is usually a B+ student because she has to find a way to balance her homework with her time practicing the clarinet. Okay, not all band girls play the clarinet. Some play the flute and others play the saxophone. There are a few who play the trombone, but frankly, a girl playing the trombone is embarrassing. This should not be tried. Ever.

At this point we should remind you that not all the girls who play in the band are First Chairs. This is true for two reasons. First of all, First Chair is someone who loves and is devoted to the band. There are other girls in band who may not share the same love and loyalty to the band. They may actually be in band because they know it is a way for them to get some easy credits. Outside of band, these girls may, in fact, make fun of the band in order to distance themselves from First Chair and the rest. These girls are not First Chairs at all. They are more like Band Traitors. A true First Chair is completely sold-out to the band and may IN FACT sit in the first chair of her instrument section. And this is where her name comes from—from these select, talented, band lovin' girls. What this means is that they have demonstrated (through competition) that they are indeed the best instrumentalist of their particular instrument in all of band and they get to sit in the first seat of their section. There is an implied honor that comes with being a literal First Chair.

Secondly, the classification First Chair pertains to any girl who finds herself wrapped up in an exclusive society or activity club that the majority of people don't understand and make fun of. Whether she's an ROTC cadet, a Choir member, a Homeschooler, or a teenage Trekkie, she is still a First Chair and all the same rules apply. Sure, The Mathlete could be considered a First Chair, but that starts to get confusing.

The life of First Chair is complicated and not always easy. Even though the ridicule and torment have served to help her figure out and to be true to herself, it is not always an easy road. She has found herself with close friends who are like her. It is not always easy feeling different from the rest of the world. The First Chair has a tendency towards harboring resentment and bitterness from being forced to put up with people who don't understand her and make fun of her. Even though she puts on a brave face and an indifferent attitude toward those who think she is a nerd, the First Chair is prone to make a mental note of those who mock her. In the back of her mind, the First Chair would like to be accepted by the normal crowd and is upset when at times she isn't. However, church is a place where First Chair often feels safe and you get to see her true colors come shining through. She is usually eager to use her musical gifts and help with music at church, whether it is playing with the worship team, playing the song during the offering time or singing in the choir. The church is a good place for First Chair to be herself. Because of her active involvement, she is well known, respected, and most importantly, has found a place where she is needed.

5 CLUES THAT YOU MIGHT BE FIRST CHAIR:

1. You own a hat too tall to wear in the car.
2. Half the pants in your closet have a stripe down the leg.
3. You know firsthand that trumpet players are good kissers. Saxophone players are not.
4. Your favorite key is C flat.
5. Anytime you begin to walk, you always lead off with your left foot.

What would you find in her locker? Sheet music, spot remover for white polyester, a spare clarinet

Email signature: "We are the music makers, and we are the dreamers of the dream. Wandering by lone sea breakers, and sitting by desolate streams. World losers and world forsakers, for whom the pale moon gleams. Yet we are movers and the shakers of the world forever it seems."

—Arthur O'Shaunessey

Favorite movie: Mr. Holland's Opus. And she cries every time.

Favorite music for chilling out: Kenny G

Favorite drink: Doesn't matter, as long as it's in the plastic cup she got at band camp that says Florida Gators Marching Band.

Shoes: Comfortable shoes for practicing marching during lunch (Reebok Princess - all white)

Website: http://www.bluedevils.org/

Picture/Posters: The University of Florida Marching Band

Makeup: Yes. She's especially good at applying her halftime "stage" makeup.

Dr. Dave's looks back at First Chair:

I was in band for a very long time; in fact, I've always been in band. I started in 5th grade. That's right, I jumped in on the very first day that I could. I just couldn't wait any longer. It's funny how excited I was about it in fifth grade. It seems that the excitement didn't wear off; graduation would've been sad, but I had the next band lined up. I proudly became a member of the band at college for another three and a half years. I was still "all about it." I couldn't get enough band. I was in symphonic band, marching band, jazz band, pep band, what the heck! Band, band, band, that's seems to have been the focus of my scholastic life. Needless to say, I've known my fair share of "band girls" throughout the eleven plus years of band.

The Drama Queen

The stage is bare, the spotlight is on, and the play is ready to begin. The crowd is hushed and waiting. With a drum roll the red velvet curtain raises to reveal the star of the show. She laughs, she cries, she shouts, she whispers. She, dear friend, is The Drama Queen. You can pick out The Drama Queen in a small group of talking girls from a good distance, provided you have decent eyesight. Even from distances of up to a half-mile, you can still spot her, though you may need to squint a little. How can you know a Drama Queen? It's not her clothes and it's not her looks. It's the way she talks. She talks not only with her mouth, but also with her hands. But her hands aren't really talking. They're waving. They're pointing. They're jabbing. They're slicing the air like a kung fu movie. She is kind of like a bird in a birdbath, flapping and chirping and splashing around. You begin to wonder what all the fuss is about. But The Drama Queen knows no boundaries when it comes to expressing herself. She is the most animated of girls, gesturing wildly when she talks. And talk, she does. A lot. If you find yourself close enough to overhear The Drama Queen's conversation, then any suspicions of this will be confirmed.

Here is an example of what you might overhear at the movie theater from The Drama Queen: "That movie was the single most awful, absolute worst movie ever made in the history of all mankind!!!" Or "That movie was the single best, most incredible, wonderfully brilliant, most genius film of all-time!!!" Here is what you'll *not* hear: "The movie was okay," or "I kinda liked that movie, sort of . . ." If you are to sit down and type out the words she will say, like we are doing, then be sure to use plenty of exclamation points!!!! The Drama Queen is really the only girl that you should do this with. She loves! exclamation points and uses them liberally! in her schoolwork and in her emails! She also uses the word *most* in every sentence. *Most* is one of those words that she mostly uses to over emphasize her point. No, always. She always uses the word *most*. Or she mostly uses the word *always*. Either way. (Other words are *really* and *totally*.) Everything in The Drama Queen's universe is black or white. Not even black or white, but rather, really, really black or really, really white. The Drama Queen is not satisfied with normal, everyday expression because she is afraid of not making her point to others. Normality and average-ness does not exist in her language. Basically, everything in her world is an exaggeration of reality.

One of the great things about The Drama Queen is that you never ever have to wonder how she is feeling. She will be either on top of the world or under it . . . and this will be quite obvious. There are several factors to consider when confronted with The Drama Queen. First there is The Nirvana factor. The Nirvana factor has nothing to do with Kurt Cobain, grunge music, or achieving a state of enlightenment. *Nirvana*, for our purpose of definition, is the ultimate experience of some pleasant emotion such as happiness or joy. This is The Drama Queen's favorite. Being happy. And when The Drama Queen is happy, she is really really really happy and a lot of fun to be around. Her joy spreads like wild fire. She is loud and funny and lets everyone around know that she is happy. There is a lot of high-pitched laughter accompanying her Nirvana. Bouncing and skipping are also known to occur. The Drama Queen loves to take the smallest good thing and turn it into a reason to throw the ultimate party, and everyone is invited. For instance, if The Drama Queen likes a particular boy and he happens to smile at her as they pass in the hallway, she immediately gathers up her closest friends and excitedly begins to plan her wedding. She is completely overjoyed and becomes the happiest of all happy people.

But what happens when something bad happens? We like to call it The Sky Is Falling factor. If the same boy (you know, the one she's going to marry) passes The Drama Queen in the hallway while talking to a friend and doesn't notice The Drama Queen, her world immediately collapses on top of her. She is devastated. There will be tears involved. No one is able to cheer her up. Instead of bouncing and skipping, there is sobbing and convulsions. She is convinced that the cute boy must certainly hate her and think she is ugly. He probably tells all his guys friends how unbelievably ugly she is and now she will never get asked to go to prom. The Drama Queen's world has come to an end and she tells her friends what she'd like her tombstone to say as she makes out her last will and testament. Her life as she knows it is over . . . but only for a short while. If, in the next class after The Sky Has Fallen, she learns that she aced the pop quiz from the day before, Nirvana returns and The Drama Queen bounces and skips to her next class with laughter following her down the hallway. Her emotions go all the way to 11 on a 1-10 scale, and she loves to make a scene.

The Drama Queen doesn't like to ride the emotional roller coaster all by herself, but instead loves to take everyone along for her ups and downs. One of the secret weapons she uses to involve people in her current state of affairs is the art of storytelling. The Drama Queen is a good storyteller and uses the most colorful descriptions. She has a way of making her life just a little bit more vivid and exciting than others, and she loves to tell all about it. As we've learned already, there will be slight (or obvious) exaggerations involved with her tales—not for the purpose of lying or being untrue, but simply to make things more interesting. Very interesting. So interesting, in fact, that you can't pull out in the middle of one of her stories. You've gotta stay to the end to hear how things turn out. She's excited and she makes you excited, too. When people are gathered around and listening intently, it's Nirvana for The Drama Queen. But once they've heard her stories a dozen times and gotten used to the colorful descriptions, slight exaggerations, and excited exclamations, they become less interested because they've heard it all before. At that point they are likely to tune out and stop listening. This is bad news for The Drama Queen and once again, The Sky Is Falling.

Another way in which she ropes people into her world is the art of whining. The Drama Queen loves to complain. If she's not hysterically happy or sullenly depressed, she complains. This is the equivalent of normalness for The Drama Queen. If Nirvana is found on a mountaintop and The Sky is Falling happens in the valley, then whining exists in a grassy meadow somewhere in between the two. If there's anything to be slightly irritated about in the world, she wants all others to know it and be as equally as irritated as she. She can continue is a state of whining for up to three days. Four, if she's really, really super whiny. Whether she

THE DRAMA QUEEN IN 5 WORDS OR LESS:

intense
melodramatic
sensational
semi-delusional
imaginative

knows it or not, this is not a quality that others enjoy, but it is one that she can't seem to shake. Another quality found in a select number of Drama Queens is that she always thinks she is sick. Anytime she sneezes, she thinks that "she has a cold coming on" or that the wart on her hand "must be cancerous" or after staring at the sun she sees spots and must be going blind. Hold on. Actually staring at the sun too long CAN make you blind! For those of you reading along at home or watching on TV, DO NOT, we repeat, DO NOT try this. Ever. And don't say we didn't warn you. But you get the picture right? The Drama Queen is sometimes a hypochondriac and loves it when others feel sorry for her. And, of course, everyone feels sorry for someone who is sick, 'cause that's just no fun.

If you are starting to think that The Drama Queen is herself no fun or a bit extreme and unlikable, please know that there are good qualities about The Drama Queen. Besides her being an awesome storyteller, one thing you can hang your hat on is that you will always know where you stand with her. If she's mad at you, she will tell you. If she's thrilled to be your friend, you can be sure that you'll hear about it. The girl wears her heart out on her sleeve and it is nearly impossible for her to cover up what she is thinking or feeling. This makes for a good friend where you can have real conversation. There's no guesswork involved. Though she can exaggerate a story, she has a hard time lying. If she tries to lie about something, her face will tell the truth every time. For whatever reason, there seems to be a giant difference between exaggerating and lying for The Drama Queen. Another great thing about The Drama Queen is that she's the queen of sensitivity. She is, of course, very sensitive to her own needs, but is also very sensitive to the needs of others. She is always willing to sit and listen to others' problems or celebrate someone else's joy.

Because of her storytelling abilities, and because of her sensitivity and flair for all things dramatic, The Drama Queen (and this is so obvious that it hurts to even say it) is usually a good actress. Yes, there we said it. Drama Queen = drama club = actress. If you go to see a play, you had better hope that the girl playing the lead role is a real life Drama Queen because then you're in for an Academy Award performance. The Drama Queen loves to act. She prefers to play the role of the most tragic character in the play or musical because *that* is a role she can really get into. And get into it, she does. You will find The Drama Queen standing in the hall between classes muttering to herself in an English accent. When you ask her what the heck she is doing, she will snap back, "SSHHHHH! Can't you SEE that I'm in CHARACTER?!" And a character she is.

Now we've talked a whole lot about the way The Drama Queen acts but not a bit about what The Drama Queen looks like; that is because we really can't tell you. The Drama Queen comes in all styles and shapes. We have not been able to pinpoint a particular style of clothes or distinguishing visual characteristics of The Drama Queen. In our lengthy study of this particular girl, we have only been able to identify her by her mannerisms. If we were to offer a calculated guess, we'd say that The Drama Queen likes to wear baggy clothes because people in the drama clubs like to wear baggy clothes. Why that is, we don't know and won't pretend like we do. That's about it.

The key to The Drama Queen is that she does not like to be alone. If The Drama Queen finds herself alone, she is uncomfortable in her own skin. She needs reassurance that she is not alone in this world and that others understand her. She needs an audience, a sympathetic audience, to make her feels comfortable with herself. It should be noted that The Drama Queen is very different than The Diva in that The Drama Queen invites/lures people's attention while The Diva expects/demands it. They both are bummed when this doesn't happen.

Oh, The Drama Queen LOVES church. Her favorite three favorite things about church are: 1. Youth group skits (she always plays the lead), 2. The annual Christmas pageant (she always plays Mary), and 3. The altar call (she always goes forward during the invitation for prayer for all her sicknesses or to repent of always stretching the truth). She also loves it when they ask if anyone wants to share their testimony because, hey, she loves to share hers.

5 CLUES that you might BE THE Drama Queen:

1. When you see a movie and say that it's the best most fantastic movie you've ever seen in your entire life, no one believes you. You say that about every movie. Whatever!

2. Every breakup is the worst breakup of all time, and you can't go on and will never be able to love again and . . . oh, who's the new guy on campus?

3. You think your life is over and your life has just begun in a span of ten minutes.

4. You religiously watch at least two soap operas. (How could Stone betray Victoria like that?!?)

5. You dream of being a famous movie star one day—you're convinced that it's your destiny.

WHAT WOULD YOU FIND IN HER LOCKER?
Pictures of every friend she has (but she is in every picture), notes from friends, a bottle of St. John's Wort

EMAIL SIGNATURE: The latest funny thing that she said and a link to her website

FAVORITE MOVIE: Legally Blonde, Breakfast at Tiffany's, Confessions of a Teenage Drama Queen

FAVORITE MUSIC: *NSYNC on a happy day, Tori Amos on a bad one

TV CHANNEL OR SHOW: The Bachelor

FAVORITE DRINK: Diet Coke

PICTURE/POSTERS: boys, boys, and more boys

AFTER SCHOOL JOB: waitress

CLOTHING LABEL: Prada

MAKEUP: waterproof mascara

Dr. Dave thinks of the Drama Queen:

Oh, the drama! It's ever so taxing on my sanity. It's like I'm a masochist. Some days I say, "WHY?! WHY?! WHY?! What have I done to myself?" Yet I wouldn't have it any other way. I know much about the drama club kind of girl . . . I married one. Rachel is her name, and everyday is full of possibilities. It might possibly be the most beautiful day ever, full of opportunity and excitement. However, I just don't know until I call home. She has so many plans and expectations for life. There is so much that she wants to do and be a part of. In the early years of our dating I often wondered, how I could fit into all the things that she was going to be doing in her life? She thrives in social situations; she feeds off of them. That's where she gets her inspiration for music, writing, and her acting. Sometimes her mood will change instantly. One time I called home, and she had been watching some television. Well, apparently Mr. Big wasn't treating Carrie so well. In Rachel's world, the smallest thing can knock the world off its axis! Now we have to spend a half an hour discussing how men are jerks, and women are stupid for putting up with such men. At least, it's not just men's fault; she admits that women are just as bad in their own right and has no misgivings about that. Rachel is a smart girl and she really thinks things out. Seriously.

THE AIRHEAD

Question: Why do airheads wear ponytails?

Answer: To hide the valve stem.

If you have just read this joke and didn't get it, you might be an airhead. Scratch that. Actually, many of you might not have understood that joke unless you are familiar with the fine art of automotive maintenance. Maybe that joke wasn't such a good idea after all. Oh, well.

Of all the girl types, The Airhead might be our favorite. Or at least the most endearing. One thing you can say about The Airhead is that she's happy. Always happy. She may even be the most agreeable girl type there is. Maybe she's always happy because she's always somewhere else. She's always a little bit behind what's going on. She can often be found staring off into space. "What's she thinking about?" you wonder as she sits with her eyes glazed over, gum perched precariously on her lower protruding lip, finger in her hair stopped mid-twirl. The world will never know, but we will never tire of trying to find out.

We love The Airhead because she's fun to laugh at . . . uh, we mean . . . with. She's the kinda girl who skips down the hall on the way to biology class, and she doesn't take biology. She's the kinda girl who finally makes a basket in gym class basketball and doesn't understand why she's the only one cheering. It doesn't matter to her that she scored for the opposing team, she's just happy she made it. And actually, this is one of our favorite things about The Airhead. She's just fun to be around because she views everything as a fun activity. She thinks everything is kinda funny. Going through the lunch line, she laughs at the entree choices. (And we will admit, lunch line crab cakes can be a somewhat funny looking.) Sitting in homeroom, she giggles at the announcements. Instead of getting mad when she drops all her books while running to class, she laughs. The Airhead is one happy girl.

The Airhead is always the same and always different. Her hobbies vary as much as The Rock Chick's hair color. This week, for instance, she believes that it's cool to enjoy photography. She overheard a friend in algebra talking about photography and decided that she too was a photographer. It's not that she wanted to be one or wanted to learn about being one. She simply was one. Is one. Has to be one. She goes to the mall and buys the most expensive camera her mom can afford, as well as all the add-ons the friendly camera guy offers. Can't skimp on the extra lenses and special film when you're a photographer! She carries her camera to school. She buys a photography book and cuts out pictures she should have shot (and is destined to shoot) and hangs them in her locker. She "shoots" on her lunch break, carefully staring into the viewfinder to capture the perfect moment . . . the perfect angle. She was born for this. It's who she is, through and through. Until next week when she realizes she was born to be a hairstylist, sells the camera on Ebay and uses the profit to buy designer shears and a box of various shades of hair color.

And speaking of hair color, we should probably address the age-old wisdom that teaches that blonde hair equals The Airhead. We've already looked at the hard scientific data (or at least our own reasonable guesswork) about Homecoming Queens and the likelihood of their blondeness, but now we turn The Airhead and her blondeness. We'll put it to you this way. Every Airhead tends to be blonde or at least appears to be so. She might have a little help from Miss Clairol. There are even some savvy Airheads that try to disguise this stereotype and color their hair from blonde to another color, but the fact still remains. Airheads are most often blonde. Hair color maintenance is high priority since the perfect hair flip is part of her flirting repertoire. The blonde hair flip is how she got her last three boyfriends. She dresses hip but not too hip, pretty much blending in with the average crowd, wearing jeans and girly tops (mostly pink) and Steve Maddens or Skechers. She mixes trends without knowing it. She wears chucks with a skirt . . . or a hoodie with a glam belt . . . and doesn't seem to realize that these accessories are mixed up. The Airhead is much harder to spot since she comes in many shapes and sizes, but you can pinpoint her once you observe her actions or hear her speak.

The Airhead doesn't fully understand universal rules that apply to everyone, like zipping up your backpack so all your books don't fall out. Or not holding a full soda can and checking your watch at the same time. Or that singing to yourself means in your head, not out loud during class. The Airhead is never successful in home ec class. She tends to leave out crucial baking ingredients, like sugar or baking soda, or accidentally sews the sleeves shut on her sewing project. It's not that she's clumsy, she just forgets or doesn't pay attention or doesn't read the directions. She might instead be thinking about how hot Johnny Depp is, instead of what the ingredients are for the baking project. She's easily distracted by pretty much anything. Especially shiny things! It's just that she's got quite a bit going on in her head and not much of it has to do with her current surroundings or companions. At a party, the Airhead becomes easier to spot. For instance, The Drama Queen makes a grand, emotional entrance. The Rock Chick quietly comes in the secret back door that requires a pass. The Homecoming Queen says hello to every single person and The Poet boycotts the whole event. But The Airhead gets lost on the way there, then drops her keys in the grass and can't figure out which door to go in. But once she arrives, she's just so happy to be there! And when she does finally walk through the front door, everyone knows it. She might announce something to everyone that makes no sense or tells a story that rambles on and on and makes no point. But for some reason, nobody seems to mind. We all just like to listen to The Airhead. She's a fun hang.

At this point we should point out that there are actually two types of Airheads. First there's The Social Airhead. The Social Airhead tends to say the wrong thing at the wrong time to the wrong person. She never means anything by it. She just says what pops into her head and is then shocked when it doesn't go over so well. The Social Airhead tends to blurt out that she doesn't like someone's new haircut or shoes or she may spill secrets accidentally, which tends to make girls really mad. We really don't care, though. Guys don't have secrets. The good part about this is that The Social Airhead accidentally tells secrets on herself, too. Whoops! Then there's The Practical Airhead, who is the girl with no common sense. She'll park in two spaces without realizing it, change lanes without signaling, or open your mail because she didn't read the name on the front. She leaves the TV, lights, and oven on, and sometimes the keys in the ignition. This is especially bad when the car is still running and all the doors are locked and she's not in it. She has also been known to stand in front of her neighbor's locker at school for ten minutes straight, trying in vain to make her locker combination work, which of course, it doesn't. The Practical Airhead is always afraid that people think she's dumb (even though she really isn't). Therefore, she watches the

Travel Channel and the Food Network and the Discovery Channel so she can learn new and interesting facts that she can share at some opportune moment. Unfortunately, she usually shares these nuggets at the most random time possible . . . like during an awkward silence. She'll inhale deeply and stare off into space while spouting off some obscure fact about whales or how candy bars are made. Then people don't think she's smart, just random.

At school The Airhead is an okay student. She probably gets all Bs on her report card. She does have a hard time paying attention in class but knows enough to study up for tests. Teachers get a little frustrated and like to call on her, not because they think she knows the answer but because they want to jar her back to attention. But in the hallways, she is usually able to get others' attention because she is prone to drop and scatter her books across the floor. Whoops! On a 1-10 scale of popularity, she ranks about 6 or 7. A lot of people know who she is because they think she is funny or amusing. Funny and amusing are not the same thing, by the way. Funny, because she might say strange things. Amusing, because her actions and activities are always entertaining. The Airhead makes for a good spectator sport.

The Airhead is also a close talker. She likes to sit RIGHT next to you and put her arm around you and look right at you. Or maybe that's the only way she can concentrate. Otherwise she starts to daydream. Drift. Lose focus. The Airhead has learned that to pay attention she has to sit close. And she might ask you to repeat yourself. A lot. You may be wondering why it seems so hard to connect with The Airhead and we sometimes wonder that, too. The reason for this is that there is an entire universe of activity going on inside her head at any given moment. While most folks like to think that she is dumb and that there is nothing going on in her brain; quite the opposite is true. She is smart and a thinker, but only small, random bits and pieces of information actually come out of her mouth. It is her lack of concise verbal communication that leads to her Airhead-ed-ness.

The Airhead is very likable and is generally happy and seems emotionally stable. To the untrained eye, she's hardly ever moody. Because of this universe of thought inside her head she is somewhat unaffected by her surroundings. She is an eternal optimist and will at first believe most anything people tell her (she's gullible). When people try and fool The Airhead (which happens a lot but isn't really all that nice) she can become the butt of people's jokes, but she's cool once she figures out what's really going on. She shrugs it off 'cause she knows that she's The Airhead.

At church, The Airhead is either on or off. By this we mean that during the worship service, she is singing away at the top of her lungs and bobbing up and down to the music. Don't be surprised if she is an intense clapper as well. She is alert and engaged. Music is good for The Airhead. But after the offering plate has been passed and the sermon is well underway, take a moment and study The Airhead. It is if a sheet has been draped over her face. She is motionless and glazed over like a warm doughnut in the display case at Krispy Kreme. Is she even conscious? That remains a matter for debate as The Airhead is once again off in another world inside her brain.

5 Clues that You Might Be The Airhead:

1. You've lost your keys seven different times . . . today.
2. You have actually lost your car before.
3. You forget to return anything and everything you borrow from your friends.
4. You repeat things constantly. Like if you're thirsty, you'll tell your friends that you're thirsty thirteen times in five minutes.
5. Staring off into space consumes a majority of your day, and you're okay with that

WHAT WOULD YOU FIND IN HER LOCKER? Ponytail holders, borrowed CDs, a retainer, a mirror to check for boogers, mid-term paper that was due last semester

EMAIL SIGNATURE: She copies whatever her smart friend has so that she'll look smart

FAVORITE MOVIE: The Freddie Prinze Jr. Collection

FAVORITE MUSIC: Punk, Jessica Simpson

TV CHANNEL OR SHOW: Reality TV, Travel Network, Food Network, Discovery Channel

FAVORITE DRINK: Sweet Tea

SHOES: The only ones she could find that morning before school.

WEBSITE: www.friendster.com

PROBABLE NICKNAMES: Bubbles

AFTER SCHOOL JOB: Can't hold a job because she's always late

CLOTHING LABEL: Wet Seal, Urban Outfitters, The Gap

MAKEUP: Drugstore and department store and make-up she borrowed from friends and forgot to return

DID YOU KNOW? . . . That baby skunks practice headstands because that is how they spray their stinky stuff. (This is an actual random fact we learned from an Airhead during an awkward pause. Her name is Jen, just in case you were wondering.)

THE GiRLFRIEND

Then there's one girl that stands out from all the rest. At least from the rest of the girls. She may list lots of girlfriends that she has, but not many girls would list her as a friend. And this is because she doesn't really hang out with them. Ever. Instead, she's permanently attached at the ankle, hip, and elbow to her boyfriend. That's right, folks. She's The Professional Girlfriend.

The Girlfriend is fairly easy to spot because she's always with her current boyfriend. Always. Meaning, always. She has gone to great lengths to somehow maneuver herself in to the same class schedule as her boyfriend. This may have involved buckets of tears and repeated trips to her guidance counselor, but she has managed to pull it off. Now she can be with her boyfriend at all times during the school day. If her particular boyfriend plays a sport, she jumps at the chance to be a cheerleader so that she can cheer for him (not the team) on the sidelines. If this boyfriend gets cut from the team for any reason, she tell the cheerleading captain that she needs to quit the squad because it is interfering with her personal life. If her boyfriend joins the French Club after school, well guess what . . . *moi aussi!*" And it should almost go without saying that The Girlfriend will do whatever it takes to be able to work the same after school job as her boyfriend. She doesn't seem to understand that there is life outside his personal space. They walk to class together, eat lunch together, sit next to each other in class, hang out after school, and go to church together. Others often fear them like some two-headed monster. But The Girlfriend shouldn't be feared. Well, except by the boyfriend should he ever try to break up with her.

The Girlfriend is overly supportive of her boyfriend, but it's not just her boyfriend that she supports. She's also finds a way to be quite involved in the lives of the boyfriend's family and close friends. She might sneak a peek at her boyfriend's calendar and write down all the birthdays of his best friends and immediate family members so that she can send them all cards. She sends his mom flowers for Mother's Day and visits his grandma in the hospital (with the boyfriend, of course). She may also go to his younger brother's Little League games or soccer matches. She is especially jazzed to be invited over to her boyfriend's house for a family dinner, particularly a family meal over the holidays like Thanksgiving or Easter brunch. In her mind, she likes to think about how "this will be just like it would be to be married," spending the holidays with *his* family. Sadly, The Girlfriend forgets to send flowers to her own mother. She can't make it her own sister's piano recital because of her boyfriend's brother's big Little League game. She even forgot her own dad's birthday once. Her family grows increasingly annoyed by her lack of attention, but she doesn't even notice. Her life and her energy are spent trying to do all she can to cement herself into the life of her boyfriend and his family.

The Girlfriend's look is not so hard to describe, but it is hard to nail down because it changes drastically with each different boyfriend. She is kind of like a chameleon that changes its color to blend into its current scene. If the current boyfriend is way into hip-hop music, The Girlfriend runs to the mall to buy a Juicy sweat suit and transforms herself into J. Lo. She may even wear a thick gold necklace with her name in rhinestones, just to be safe. If she is a hip-hipster, she must consider the bling-bling factor. If the current boyfriend is a skateboarder, she will save her money to buy new trucks and wheels, and outfit herself in anything Tony Hawk might wear. If the boyfriend is a gamer, then she buys an Xbox and so is she. You get the picture. She doesn't really fit into one particular group of people but will try her best. Her look and her life will change to match that of the boyfriend.

Her identity is to be his other half. It doesn't matter what she likes or doesn't like because what she *really* likes is being with her boyfriend and it's her full-time job.

Like we mentioned earlier, The Girlfriend also has lots of girls who she considers her best friends. She's constantly making fun plans with these friends, and then constantly breaking them at the last minute to be with her boyfriend. These friends are usually mad at The Girlfriend and will talk about her behind her back. The

> **THE GIRLFRIEND IN 5 WORDS OR LESS:**
> chameleon
> needy
> affectionate
> supportive
> clingy

Girlfriend has no idea about all this and thinks they are all as close as close friends can be . . . even though she never spends time with them. Even though she forgets their birthdays and forgets to call and stands them up. Yet, every time The Girlfriend breaks up with her boyfriend, she runs to these friends, cries a swimming pool full of tears and says that she's sorry she hasn't been a better friend and promises that it won't ever happen again. She is sooooo thankful that they are always there for her, but they are sooooo confused by her flakiness.

The Girlfriend lives in constant fear that her boyfriend will leave her. This feeling haunts her. Therefore, she usually has a really good guy friend as a backup. Just in case. This back up is usually a good friend of her boyfriend or one of her older brother's friends. A nice safe guy friend who's there in case of emergency. She will expend a little time and energy into this relationship to keep him around and interested. Unfortunately, the backup is a guy who secretly likes The Girlfriend and is hoping that one day he may move up the relational ladder to official boyfriend status. But he never will. He's the backup. Someone should let him in on this little secret so he can move on.

With The Girlfriend, it seems inevitable that the dreaded and feared day will indeed come. The day of the breakup. The breakup usually occurs when the current boyfriend has had just about all he can take of The Girlfriend. (Keep in mind that The Girlfriend never breaks up. That would be unthinkable. It's the boyfriend who does the breaking.) He feels smothered, suffocated, and substantially subdued by the constant attention and companionship that The Girlfriend lavishes on him, and it becomes too much to deal with any longer. He may try to give her the "It's not you; it's me" speech or the "I just want to be friends" talk, but in the end, the current boyfriend musters up the courage and eventually breaks up with The Girlfriend. When this happens, you do not want to anywhere nearby because all the screaming monkeys of fire and brimstone will fly forth from her ears and wreak havoc on your sanity. You have never seen crying and wailing like this before.

And can you blame her? She has invested herself so completely in her now ex-boyfriend's life that she is like a pen without paper, like a lake without water, like a hippie without a tie-dye shirt. Everything is wrong and there's no way to fix it. There will be a period of a few days when she . . . (gulp) . . . doesn't . . . have . . . a . . . boyfriend. During these days she will cling to her dear friends and wander aimlessly searching for her new identity. Her new boyfriend. She is lost and doesn't seem to know exactly who she is anymore. But then it happens. She meets somebody new. And her life can begin again. Another boyfriend, someone waiting to have his picture taken with her and his letter jacket borrowed and his grandma visited.

Another way of looking at the girlfriend would be that she is the type of girl that just cannot be alone. Not even for a few seconds. She is the girl that forms her identity through being with someone else but struggles through life because without a boyfriend she feels like nothing. It is not that she *is* nothing, but that she hasn't figured out a way to go through life without having a guy on her arm to lead the way.

The Girlfriend is well versed in many of the different Christian denominations and has attended multiple churches: Baptist, Methodist, Lutheran, Roman Catholic, Assemblies of God, Church of God, Church of Christ, Church of God in Christ, Interdenominational, Nondenominational. Why? Because The Girlfriend has regularly attended her many different boyfriends' churches and become quite accustomed to their ways, though she's never been at one place long enough for her to consider it her home. She has enjoyed them all and has made it a point to fit right in.

5 CLUES THAT YOU MIGHT BE THE GIRLFRIEND:

1. You refer to yourself as "we" or "us." (ex. We loved that movie . . . we hate broccoli . . .)

2. If your boyfriend goes out of town on a family vacation, you feel lightheaded and have to lie down . . . for the entire week. You remind him that next time they should bring you along so that this doesn't happen again.

3. Your friends always seem to be mad at you and you don't know why. You keep meaning to call them but forget because you are always with your boyfriend.

4. During class, you doodle your first name with your current boyfriend's last name and daydream about what you'll name your kids.

5. You have boxes full of pictures, stuffed animals, and letters from old boyfriends. You can't bear to throw out any of it.

What Would You Find in Her Locker?

A framed 5x7 of her boyfriend, 27 snapshots of her and her boyfriend, dried roses that she saved from her boyfriend, a love note left by her boyfriend

Email Signature: "It's better to have loved and lost than never to have loved at all."

Favorite Movie: Whatever her boyfriend's favorite movie is

Favorite Music: Whatever music her boyfriend likes

TV Channel or Show: Whatever he's watching

Favorite Drink: Whatever he's drinking

Shoes: If her boyfriend is on the short side, she puts all her heels away.

Website: *www.theknot.com* (dreaming of the future!)

Probable Nicknames: Pookie

Clothing Label: Her boyfriend's letter jacket

Makeup: As much or as little as her boyfriend prefers.

Brian Pittman's
fond memories of
THE GIRLFRIEND:

Girlfriends. What can I say? There is nothing better than having a good girlfriend. There is nothing worse than having a bad one either. Well, actually, getting eaten by a shark is worse than having a bad girlfriend I bet. I will use someone else's example rather than my own because I have no girlfriend. I knew a guy named Matt. He and his girlfriend Megan were always together. They are actually engaged right now and I see them around. It is good to see they are still going strong. Megan seems to always take care of Matt. Supportive in every way. They always seemed to have like interests, and she seemed like the type that a mom would love to be with her son. (I don't know that for sure, though. How could I? I am not a mom.) Megan was always loyal to Matt, and anyone who was around just knew these two were meant to be together.

Vanilla Pudding

She's as sweet as she sounds and just as interesting and fascinating. She's not as rich as Tiramisu, she's not as tangy as a Lemon Tart, she's not as complicated as a White Chocolate Hazelnut Cheesecake, or as exotic as Walnut Baklava. As far as a dessert goes, she's regular Vanilla Pudding . . . not too crazy and not too bland. No one complains about vanilla pudding because it's sweet and tasty and a part of the fabric of this great country. Bill Cosby likes vanilla pudding and so do little kids. So does everyone in-between. She is like a comfort food, a staple, and something that you would find in anyone's cupboard. It's the perfect complement to nearly every meal, handy and never troublesome. But let's stop talking about food because it will get confusing and we will get hungry. For our purposes, Vanilla Pudding isn't really a smooth and creamy dessert. She's a girl. She is a nice, normal, average girl. She's the proverbial girl next door.

So who is this girl? We have looked at the eleven other types of girls and learned that they can be a number of wildly different things. They can be happy (The Homecoming Queen) or they can be moody (The Rock Chick). They can require attention (The Drama Queen) or they are satisfied with a smaller circle of friends (First Chair). They can be driven (The Overachiever) or they can be passive (The Girlfriend). They can be smart (The Mathlete) or they can appear clueless (The Airhead). They can also be a jock (The Athlete), a trendsetter (The Diva), or a girl with a cause (The Poet). So where does this leave Vanilla Pudding? Right in the middle. The average. The all-American, normal girl. She has qualities of all the other girls types listed above, but none of these qualities are to an extreme. And we must bring her to your attention lest you get the impression that we think all girls are so obvious and predictable. We know they're not. The female gender is so complex and no one girl perfectly fits any one category. But Vanilla Pudding will be our designation of the average, laid-back girl.

VANILLA PUDDING IN 5 WORDS OR LESS:

normal
even keel
friendly
fun

We like to think that Vanilla Pudding is normal because she is the girl who we most identify with. This girl is as close to a boy as they come. And we don't mean that is a weird or unflattering way. Normal, for a girl, is being a lot like a boy, only prettier and smells nice. Well, she's not *like* a boy per se, but she isn't so emotional all the time. We don't ever witness her wild mood swings or feel the wrath of her temper. She doesn't freak out unless it's called for. This girl is "steady eddy" and is predictable. The normal girl is also into things that we boys like—like sports, music, video games, and maybe professional wrestling and monster truck rallies. Well, maybe not those last two, but you catch the drift. If a girl is into the same things that boys are into, we find that we can relate to her better. We have things to talk about, and she is comfortable to be around. Another thing we like is that Vanilla Pudding is always there whether we pay attention to her or not. She laughs at our jokes and cries in the right places at the movies. She helps us with our homework and listens to us talk about the hot girl we like. Vanilla Pudding is our friend. Most times we don't think about her like we would The Homecoming Queen or The Diva because those are the girls we want to date. But oddly enough, when the time comes, this is the girl that we might someday marry (except for Dave, who married a Drama Queen)—that is if she hasn't already married a doctor or successful lawyer. Then it will be too late for us and that'd serve us right for waiting around.

Vanilla Pudding enjoys life and loves to get the most out of it that she can. She is adventurous without being a daredevil. She enjoys a good hike or being outdoors and doesn't mind getting dirty once in a while. (Guys love to get dirty . . . when we were kids, mud and sticks were our favorite toys.) She is funny and loves a good joke. She can tell one, too. She loves a good book or movie. She loves her little brother and sister. She loves ice cream. Vanilla Pudding has a positive outlook on life and that makes her good to be around. She can always lift your spirits. She remembers to send her friends birthday cards and will buy her girlfriends flowers if they are feeling down. At Christmas, she goes shopping at the mall and is a "Secret Santa" to a couple underprivileged kids. Vanilla Pudding is thoughtful and compassionate. She's a B+ student. Not too smart and definitely not dumb. Vanilla Pudding is not too skinny, not too fat. She's not the most trend-conscious person, but always looks comfortable in jeans and a sweater. She prefers a "classic" look. Other than that, we have found her amazingly hard to describe.

Vanilla Pudding is right at home in church. She loves Jesus and is willing to serve him anyway she can. She appreciates her church and youth group but is not necessarily a leader unless she is called upon to do so. She is, in almost every single way, the average girl. And when we say average, we mean it in the best way possible.

5 CLUES THAT YOU MIGHT BE VANILLA PUDDING:

1. You have lots of guy friends, but rarely have a boyfriend.
2. If you took a personality test, you would probably be a "Golden Retriever."
3. You are well liked by most other girl types.
4. You shop at the Gap.
5. You like meat AND potatoes.

What Would You Find in Her Locker? Books, pictures of friends, notes, a jacket

Email Signature: Just her name and "Have a great day!"

Favorite Movies: chick flicks, dramas, action movies—a little of everything

Favorite Music: Top 40

TV Channel or Show: MTV, Friends, ER

Favorite Drink: Coke

Website: www.amazon.com, www.ebay.com, www.friendster.com

Picture/Posters: Pictures of Orlando Bloom cut out of US Weekly

Probable Nicknames: Buddy

After School Job: The Gap

Clothing: The Gap, Old Navy, Kohl's, Target

Makeup: Maybelline, Bonne Bell, Revlon

Matthew Hoopes on
VaniLLa PuDDing:

Beth was a few years older than me, and I don't really ever remember talking to her until my freshman year, because at that point we were both in the same section of youth group . . . senior high." I remember feeling so old and mature, but at the same time very small and not as cool as the older kids. But Beth was a good girl; she was easy to talk to and always initiated conversation, which was good for me because I was pretty shy. Beth was the classic church girl and was totally involved in the youth group, and I think she found a lot of her identity there, and especially with her friends. She may have not been the most popular girl at school (and I don't mean to say that in a mean way, but she just wasn't the cheerleader type and was not really worried about style or status). She was so nice though, and always thought about other people, tried to include them, and was friends with anyone. That is something that I really respected about her, and I wanted to be outgoing and sure of myself like her. I am not saying that she was perfect, but certainly a model Christian and some-one that I tried to be like. She loved the Lord, and you could just tell because of the way she did everything that she did.

I think I was most impressed by how she so quickly invited my friends and I to be friends with her and her friends (who I was mostly too embarrassed to talk to because I had a crush on some of them). But this was just way different than anyone I had met at school, and she totally treated me as an equal and always told me how cool I was and how I had neato shoes and stuff like that. She was very complimentary and you could really tell that it wasn't fake and she wasn't trying to manipulate anyone . . . but that she was just very encouraging. Beth was on the ministry team and was one of the leaders of the youth group. She would help plan events and even when she wasn't doing that, she was planning group trips to the mall and out to dinner after.

I AM UNDERSTOOD?

Boy Types

As you have seen, there are quite a number of different types of girls out there. We counted twelve. And there might be a few more types of girl that we didn't even know about before we wrote this book. If you are someone who we missed earlier in the book, we're sorry and we'd like to meet you someday. Anyway, you can see that we have done our best to investigate all the kinds of girls we could think of, and we realize that the world of girls is really complex because girls come in all different shapes and sizes with different moods, personalities, interests, and looks. While this is not very surprising (and is to be expected from the fairer, more mysterious sex), you may be amazed to learn that there are different types of boys, too. Guys are far simpler and easier to figure out, though. And we should know because we are boys ourselves and experts in this field as we have been boys all our lives. Here is a brief description of the first type of boy . . . .

THE APE

t is the middle of summer break, and the alarm clock turns 11:00 a.m. He is still in bed, mouth slightly ajar, with a rather large drool stain on the pillow outlining his head like some sort of creepy halo. The noise being emitted from his mouth and nostrils is the sound of monsters and other comic book creatures. After repeated attempts to wake him, his mother gives up and leaves him to rot in his filth. Sometime in the early afternoon, his eyes crack open into bleary little slits, his hair shooting into a thousand different directions all at once when he finally rolls out of bed and onto a floor covered in crushed potato chips, gum wrappers, comic books, and dirty socks. After lying there momentarily, he pulls himself up onto two feet, finds a wadded up t-shirt in the corner and sniffs it for offensive odors. If he discovers none, he pulls it on. He repeats the same procedure with a pair of old nasty jeans and now he is ready to begin what's left of his day. Behold! In all his majesty, we present to you . . . The Ape.

The Ape looks just about like he sounds. For The Ape, his appearance is all about convenience and ease. He doesn't care so much about dressing up or looking good for anyone or anything. A baseball hat is a good enough excuse to not wash his hair. Chewing gum is his excuse for not brushing his teeth. You may find copious amount of dirt under his fingernails—the same nails that haven't been cut in over a month. Even the simple things, like tying his shoelaces, are more trouble than they're worth. Even if he trips over his shoelaces and falls down on the sidewalk, he would probably just end up with a big, bloody gash to add to his growing collection of scars. He would appreciate that. It is almost a certainty that his mom does all his laundry and cleans up his room when he's not there. What's worse is that he may even get mad at his mom for cleaning up after him because "now he can't find all his stuff." He is a messy guy who doesn't seem to care.

The first rule of The Ape is that he prefers to stay up as late as humanly possible, followed by sleeping as long as is allowed by law. As we mentioned, this method works well for the summertime but is hard to maintain during the school year and it frustrates The Ape. You might say that he is lazy, but this is only partially true. There are many things that The Ape pursues with much energy and passion. The following list may help you to identify The Ape's primary pursuits:

Sports

Okay. This may seem obvious, but it must be mentioned. Sports are one of the many ways in which The Ape either gets himself wound up or winds down. He may participate or he may only watch. It doesn't matter which, because boys love their sports. And by sports we mean games that involve the probability of some type of physical contact. Football, American style, consists of a bunch of beefy guys in protective pads running around and bashing each other hard. This is an excellent example of sports. Football, European style, consists of less protective padding (which is good), but they rarely make contact with each other, minus the occasional kick to the shins (also good). Other Ape sports worth mentioning are boxing (for obvious reasons), skateboarding (for the likelihood of a gnarly wipeout), hockey (when they throw down their gloves, something crazy is about to happen), NASCAR races (flaming crashes are always thrilling, unless someone really gets hurt) and miniature golf. Okay. We were kidding about that last one. Ping-pong, which is an officially sanctioned Olympic "sport" and is considered a sport by many, is not a sport at all and much be avoided by Apes at all costs. The only exclusion to the sports=contact rule is poker. We can't give you a reason for this, but Apes seem to like their poker.

Contests of Stupidity
(otherwise known as The Dare)

There has recently been an MTV program that was wholly dedicated to Apes and their dares. The show is no longer on the air, but featured an Ape named Johnny Knoxville and his group of other Apes, who would concoct a dangerous or moronic stunt and then proceed to dare each other to complete it. This would almost always result in welts, bruises, scratches, and an assortment of other injuries. Dare an Ape to do anything, and he will probably go ahead and try it. Silly Ape. We won't go into any detail about all that except to say that Apes really seem to like this sort of thing. Another thing that The Ape likes that is sort of related to this subject is his scars. Anytime The Ape has a wound or injury that leaves a permanent mark, he is filled with pride at his "accomplishment." The Ape probably didn't intent to maim himself, but he is prideful as though he did. Scars are like a badge of honor for The Ape, and he especially loves to retell the story of each of his scars, whether or not anyone else cares to listen. Girls do not like this type of storytelling and will usually get up and leave The Ape even before he has a chance to finish.

Video Games

The Ape is also known for his proclivity of video games. He likes the shoot 'em up games that involve shooting gangsters or deer the most, but he will also spend hours at night building the perfect SIM City. He may also be prone to play video game sports like football or basketball and dream that he is a super star athlete while sitting in a recliner chair with a bag of Doritos on his lap and a half consumed two-liter of Coke on the floor. When The Ape plays video games, his ability to communicate is impaired by the flashing screen, and he is left to mutter inarticulate, exclamatory statements like "grrrimeneypete," "whoatherenelly," and "whydontyalookatthatnow" while smashing his thumbs repeatedly on the controller. He is far, far away in another universe, and it is hopeless to ask a question and receive a well-reasoned response. Don't even bother.

Music

The Ape loves music but not all sorts of music. His is only the music that can be listened to at super loud volume which leaves him with only two genres at his disposal. Rock and roll and Hip-hop. There are no other musical styles that can (or should) be listened to at loud volumes. Country, classical, jazz, and pop music are not made to be listened to at volumes that exceed the level of normal everyday conversation. Would you want to have your conversation drowned out by the twang of Keith Urban's guitar or by the shrill strings of Wagner's "Night on Bald Mountain"? Mile Davis's "Kind Blue" turned all the way "to eleven"? We think not. Would you listen to Brittany Spears at all? We hope not! The Ape, if he has enough money, will also buy the loudest possible stereo for his car, to rumble his trunk with hip-hop or shatter the back window with some good old-fashioned monster rock. A good way to pick out an Ape is if you *hear* his car stereo before you can actually *see* him coming down the street. That is always a sure sign of an Ape spotting.

Movies

The Ape's preference of movies follows that of his video games. The more explosions, car chases, and blood, the better. You will never hear an Ape say: "What a compelling film that was. I was particularly fond of the in-depth character development and the dialog between the lead actors. The tension between them was simply palpable." Instead, you will most likely hear "Man, dude, I wish there were like more explosions and stuff!"

Monkey Bars
(or The Ape's hang)

The Ape enjoys the company of other Apes. Even when he is in a dating relationship (yes, some Apes do have girlfriends), he will often opt out of a date with "his girl" (yes, he uses a possessive pronoun to refer to his girlfriend) so that he can hang out and do dumb stuff with others of his gender and type. Sometimes referred to as male bonding, it seems as though all guys must have a certain amount of time spent with other guys in order to function properly. This is a sacred thing to Apes and not to be trifled with, but we will write more on this subject later. Ladies, pay attention. The Ape requires hanging out with other apes. If this need is not met, he may become a real pain.

Various Ape Interests

- Apes like dogs, not cats. Dogs will run around, bring you stuff, and lick your face. Cats are just too snobby.

- Apes enjoy spitting a lot—just for the heck of it. This makes watermelon and sunflower seeds among their most favorite foods.

- Firecrackers/Fireworks. Again, anything that explodes is cool.

- Transportation. Cars or motorcycles. The faster and louder, the better. The Ape thinks that bicycles, walking, and other forms of environmentally friendly transportation are for sissies.

- Bad humor. Any joke about human waste and other crude topics are a favorite. This activity may also include trying to burp out the alphabet and laughing hysterically while trying to light the blue flame. (If you don't know what this means, never mind.)

- Pranks. The Ape loves to play jokes on others. Crank calls, whoopee cushions, and well-placed water balloons are only a small fraction of his total prank arsenal. He likes to laugh at other people.

As you can see, The Ape's interests revolve around macho activities that display his bad humor, his strength, his bravery, and his aggressiveness but not anything that would show his emotional side. The Ape figures that being emotional is for girls.

Girls

Ah, speaking of girls, there is another thing that The Ape does care about. The Ape likes girls. But unfortunately, a lot of Apes really don't like to *talk* to girls; instead, they just leer at them and talks about how HOT girls are with other Apes. Remember, Apes like to *look* at girls and talk *about* girls. Ladies, pay particular attention to this: The Ape has a problem and that is, when it comes to females, they like to *look* at females and *think* about females and *talk* about females but not always in the most wholesome of ways. Apes tend to have *one* thing on their minds. And lest you haven't figured out what we're talking about, we're talking about The Ape's preoccupation with sex. This doesn't just apply to fifteen-year-old Ape boys who are just starting their journey to become men; it also applies to Apes of *any* age.

If an Ape can gather enough thought to figure out what a girl wants to hear, he will often say it. He does this almost without thinking and pays no attention to whether he means a single word of it or not. We strongly advise that you be careful with anything that comes out of the Ape's mouth, be it sunflower seeds, romantic phrases, or whatever.

Relationships

The Ape is also easy to spot when it comes to his relationships. If The Ape has a girlfriend, but he knows he must break up with her, he won't do it. Instead of ending things when he knows that it's time, he just starts acting like a complete jerk so that his girlfriend will have no choice but to end the relationship. He does this so that he will look like the good guy and so he can say, "Well, she broke up with me."

The Ape is also renowned for his inability to commit. It is the classic "he loves you, he loves you not" scenario. On Sunday night, he hugs you and says that he likes you and has never met another woman like you. Monday at lunch, he says he doesn't think you are attractive "like that," and he doesn't like you "like that." But then he whines because it's "so difficult to say good-bye." Then Tuesday he calls and asks what happened to the two of you and wonders why it didn't work out. The Ape is also entirely unable to match his actions to his words. He says he likes you. He doesn't call. He says he can't wait to talk to you again. He doesn't call. He shows up at your job and hugs you and smells your hair. He doesn't call.

The Ape is also very insecure. He's so busy being macho and proving to his friends that he's a "man's man" that he doesn't know how to interact with girls. He bugs his best guy friend about hooking him up with a girl, and when his friend does, he doesn't know how to act around the girl. He might try to take her out on a date but instead of talking to her and getting to know her, he calls all his friends on his cell phone and drives too fast and forgets his wallet—leaving his date to pay for dinner and the movie.

He is often unwilling to branch out or accept change. He may also harass the girls he likes because he is a second-grader stuck in a man's body. He thinks that way he does things is perfectly fine and sees no reason to change it whatsoever. These are only some of the ways you can know an Ape in relationships. Hopefully by now you get the picture.

Now we don't want to paint the wrong picture of The Ape. While The Ape is lazy, uncultured, rude, self-serving, and may easily say the first thing that pops into his head, he is also fairly loveable in an immature, kid brother sort of way. He will irritate you one minute, and the next will have you spraying milk through your nose because you're laughing so hard. Apes are often funny like that and that's why it's hard to hate The Ape.

So to wrap up, The Ape is a bit on the self-centered side of things. For being such a general mess, it is almost comical that he thinks more highly of himself than he should. He doesn't tend to look out for others but only himself. He wants to feel good about himself and will find ways to do this at other people's expense. This is the default condition of nearly all guys. Poor Ape. Poor, poor Ape.

MR. WONDERFUL

Now that we taken a long hard look at The Ape, it's time to introduce you to the other type of guy. He is a real doll, and we shall call him Mr. Wonderful. To do our best in bringing this other guy type to your attention, we have done hours of scientific research, conducted interviews, and read a few magazines. What we have discovered is the perfect male—the guy you want to bring home to meet your family. As you read this description, you will find it hard to believe that such a guy exists. But he does. Well, sort of . . .

Mr. Wonderful has dark brown, black, or blond hair with brown or blue eyes. We're sorry to all the redheaded guys with green eyes out there, but you don't seem to fit the description of Mr. Wonderful. Anyway, Mr. Wonderful is usually 5'8" or taller, is somewhat muscular, and has the perfect tan or color of skin. His weight is in proportion to his height—he's not too skinny, not too fat. He has a nice smile and straight white teeth. He may even have dimples and "good lips" (whatever that means). His face is void of acne though he may have a few well-placed freckles. His hair and his breath always smell good. He has a nice sounding voice and a "cute" laugh. He dresses sharply and overall is very handsome.

In addition to his staggering good looks, Mr. Wonderful is athletic, but he knows that the world doesn't exist for sports alone. He enjoys going to sports events but also volunteers his time at a retirement home. Mr. Wonderful is hard working and has clear direction for his life. He has a good job and owns his own car. He has hopes and dreams of who and what he might become someday, but he's not too driven to make a name for himself. He cares about the things that are wrong in this world and wants to help right injustice. Mr. Wonderful loves both dogs *and* cats. He also loves his mom, dad, sisters, and brothers. He also loves his church and his country. He is outgoing and popular, but not too popular. He isn't shy or conceited. He is intelligent and polite but very funny as well. Even when he is being funny or telling a good joke, it is never at anyone else's expense. It should go without saying that he has never been in trouble with the law and, for that matter, he doesn't smoke, drink, or curse. He is super smart and does well in school. He can spell. Mr. Wonderful has good values and morals, is creative, and loves animals. He likes children, picnics, and has impeccable table manners. Mr. Wonderful seems to be a dreamy guy.

But wait . . . it only gets better. If there is a girlfriend in Mr. Wonderful's world, he treats her like a princess. He is affectionate and calls her cute pet names like "baby," "beautiful," etc. He is sweet to her in both public and in private. Mr. Wonderful always compliments her and always remembers special days like anniversaries and birthdays. Sometimes he even sends her flowers for no particular reason. He is spontaneous and will come by to see her unexpectedly or will call her just to say "hi" or to hear the sound of her voice. He leaves notes on her car or in her locker or charming voicemails and text messages on her phone. He carries pictures of her in his wallet and backpack and will doodle her name on his notebook—and he's not embarrassed that he does it. Mr. Wonderful likes to take walks with her just so he can hold her hand. He also remembers each time to hold the door open for her, especially the car door. He communicates what he is thinking or feeling. Mr. Wonderful is sensitive, and he apologizes when he is wrong. He doesn't talk to other girls more than her, but he does talk to his guy friends about her all the time—to the point where they've had just about enough. He will tell her that he misses her when we're not together. He can always make her laugh. Mr. Wonderful is also a great listener and never interrupts her when she is talking, and it makes her feel like she is the center of his world, which she is.

Mr. Wonderful likes to shop with his girlfriend, and he buys her nice things. He likes to take her out dancing, which is one of those things that The Ape won't do, but Mr. Wonderful is smooth on his feet. He is also smooth because he writes her poetry or songs, and he can cook the most exquisite meals. He likes to play board games with her (he lets her win) or puts puzzles together (he lets her put in the last piece). Mr. Wonderful enjoys long walks on the beach and will watch chick flicks with his girl and not complain. He just wants to be with her as much as possible.

Mr. Wonderful is thoughtful enough to never stare at other girls, and he doesn't make her cry. He doesn't play mind games with her and never raises his voice at or around her. He doesn't lie or cheat on her. He doesn't even do those small irritating things like saying sorry all the time when it's not needed or pointing out her imperfections. He likes to comfort her when she's sad. He is trustworthy, committed, patient, persistent, punctual, and romantic.

Wow, what a guy. He is so perfect and it kinda makes us tired just thinking about what a swell guy he can be. Do you know a Mr. Wonderful? If you can't think of one off-hand, don't you wish you knew him? Well, chances are you do. Here is a shocker for you: Every guy on the planet is Mr. Wonderful, but only on a part-time basis. For that matter, every single guy on the planet is also The Ape, but again, only on a part-time basis. What we are really trying to say is this: All guys are the same and each has the potential to be both The Ape and Mr. Wonderful at the same time . . . a strange and beautiful mix of self-centered slob and selfless gentleman. So when a guy shows up on *your* doorstep, you may not immediately know exactly who has come calling, The Ape or Mr. Wonderful. Give it a little time and observe him closely and you will be able to figure it out.

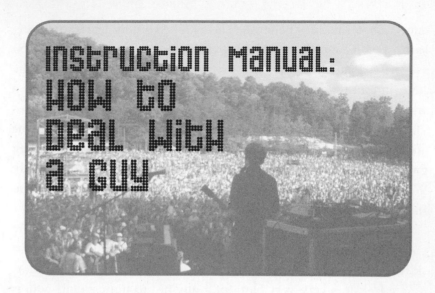

INSTRUCTION MANUAL: HOW TO DEAL WITH A GUY

Since all guys are both The Ape and Mr. Wonderful, we thought we'd take a moment to write you a little instruction manual on how to deal with a guy. We don't want to give too much away, however, because some of the best things in life will be discovered on your own. But here are some of the highlights.

Guys like to be needed. It doesn't really so much matter how, we just do. Whether it is to walk you out to your car after a late night movie or to watch your stuff while you go to the ladies room, or pick up the pencil you dropped, we want you to need us for anything. Well, anything that doesn't involve our emotions or "sharing." When you say that you need us for this or for that, we begin to feel important. It's important for us to feel important.

Guys like to be asked out. This is the next step beyond being needed. Now, you *want* to spend time with us. This is even better. We wrote a song once about being asked to the Sadie Hawkins

113

dance. There's nothing better than being asked out by a girl. Sure, sure, sure . . . you are probably thinking that it is the *guy's* responsibility to ask the *girl* out, right? Don't worry, we will ask you out most of the time, but all we are saying is that it's nice to be asked out once in a while, too.

Give compliments. Guys like to be complimented. It could be about how nice we look or if we're behaving ourselves. Remember, guys are kind of simple, and if we are acting a lot more like Mr. Wonderful rather than The Ape, you should tell us. Positive reinforcement goes a long way for a simpleminded guy.

Guys love and hate short skirts and plunging necklines. But before you go thinking that we are advocating that girls should wear short skirts and tight shirts, think again. We are simply stating an unfortunate fact. It is very, very hard for a guy not to notice a girl who is dressed . . . well, barely dressed. Remember in our discussion of The Ape that guys like to look at girls. But also remember that the Mr. Wonderful in all of us feels very uncomfortable around the scantily clad ladies. Our Mr. Wonderfulness is very conscious of the bad reputation that The Ape has given all males, so we want it to be known that we are working very hard not to give in to our barbarian Ape instincts. We guys are not supposed to think wrong thoughts about you girls, and we take responsibility when we do, but some of you make it hard for us to keep our minds out of the gutter with some of the things you wear. This is probably our #1 weakness.

Guys are, without exception, visual creatures, and somehow, many of you girls have figured out that you are able to get our attention quicker and more easily if you wear something sparse. The problem with this is that you are appealing to us as an object of desire and not as a person. You are not inviting us to get to know you; you are simply showing off your "merchandise." We believe that most times there is a direct correlation between the degree of a girl's immodest dress and the lack of a her self-worth and confidence or just complete ignorance. You are a little more important and valuable than that . . . to become some guy's sexual fantasy or prey. So be smart about what you wear. Guys appreciate a sense of mystery. If we don't know what you're thinking and you're not telling us, you've got us right where you want us. We would prefer if you not emotionally vomit on our shoes and tell us every little thing about you. Keep us guessing. Mysterious girls will get us every time.

Guys don't like girls who are taller than them. We wish we could explain why, but that's just the way it is. It takes a real man to go out with a girl who's taller than him. So if you're ever in doubt about how tall the guy is you like, just leave those tall, clunky shoes at home in the closet. If you realize that you're still taller than the guy, try bending ever so slightly at the knees and slump your shoulders a bit. The extra two inches of height he will gain may make all the difference.

Guys don't like it when girls don't laugh at their jokes. It's not that we dislike you if you don't laugh at our jokes, but it is a blow to our self-esteem. We try very hard to make you laugh. In fact, this is our best bait to see if you like us—if we can make you laugh. Even if we're failing miserably, try and muster up a courtesy laugh for us. That will help us out a lot. Thank you.

We said earlier that guys like girls who are mysterious. It is still true, however, that girls who are *too* quiet make us nervous. Even if you think of yourself as painfully shy, please try to hold a conversation with us. If girls are too quiet, we automatically think that you don't like us at all. Unless you desperately want us to leave you alone, talk to us. Otherwise, your timidity will scare us away.

Guys don't like girls who are too needy. (This is not the same as being needed, by the way.) Girls who are needy make guys crazy, and we want to run screaming away to the nearest monster truck rally for a strong dose of testosterone. We actually know a guy who got a call one night from a friend-girl who was all crying and screaming. She told him that she was standing on the kitchen table and was begging him to come over and kill a giant bug in her apartment. She lived a half an hour away from him, but the poor sucker got in his car and drove all the way to her apartment. Sure enough, a half hour later when he arrived, he found her sitting cross legged on her kitchen table, but the bug was nowhere in sight. It figures. This kind of thing makes guys nuts.

Guys don't like girls who are too aggressive either. We figure that it is our job to be aggressive and when a girl comes on too strong, we head for the door. Like we said earlier, it's good for you to ask us out on occasion, but don't make demands on us. Guys like to be in the driver's seat and think that we are calling the shots—even if we're not. Remember, again, guys like a little mystery.

Here's something that most guys can't figure out: toe rings. Why do girls put rings on their toes? Sure, toes are the fingers of your feet but why are girls so obsessed with them? We're not really sure what the point is of dressing up your toes and adorning them with rings, paint, and even French manicures. It's like you admire your feet. This is a strange thought to a guy. Guys strictly think of their feet as utilitarian. Feet are meant to stand on. You kick stuff with your feet. Feet can become, shall we say, a little funky smelling at times. As a rule for guys, feet are meant to be kept under wraps. If we didn't know better, we would think that you are so pleased with your feet that you throw parties for them when we are not looking. But for the life of us, we have no idea why.

One last thing . . . Going back to what we were saying a little while ago. Ladies, you know those low-rise jeans that you wear? Here's a little tip just for you. If the circumference around your hips exceeds that of the waistband of the jeans you are wearing, please go home and change clothes immediately. We have seen far too much Krispy Kreme spilling over the tops of girls' jeans. This looks gross and ridiculous. Also, you may want to consider how low your low-rise jeans go. Nobody wants to see a girl's plumber's . . . er, um, backside.

This is wrong and quite unattractive. We know that we are not any sort of fashion police, but some things are so obvious that we just had to say *something*.

So there you go. We hope this little manual has been helpful to you. Hopefully now you know a little more about guys and what in the world we are thinking.

when you're around

Relationships

TiME BOMBS: GiRL ReLationsHiPS

By now I think we've all learned that there are many, many different types of girls. Therefore, when you put these types together, magic can happen. Well, maybe not magic. Maybe it's just combustion with lots of sparks and lip gloss. There are all sorts of different relationships when girls get together; some are to be expected and some are simply unfathomable. Here are some observations from a guy's rock and roll perspective on you girls and the peculiar relationships you have with each other.

Acquaintances

Insider Tip: Acquaintances are not *really* friends. This means Acquaintances cannot truly be classified as one of the many girl relationships. But we all have them. Lots of them. So we figured we ought to briefly look into this Girl-Acquaintance situation before delving into the wonder that is the girl relationship.

For a girl, an Acquaintance could be just about any girl that is seen or encountered somewhat frequently without any intimate details being shared. There is a level of familiarity with The Acquaintance that is typically accompanied by a feeling that you *should* know more about her than you really do. A good sign that a girl is an Acquaintance and not an actual friend is that you know her first name but not her last. You might share a class with her, run into her at your local coffee hangout, or see her at the movies. Because of the familiarity that comes with The Acquaintance, you'll probably acknowledge her presence with a slight wave, a half-muttered hello, or a quick smile-and-a-nod. But you certainly don't know her well enough to holler across a crowded restaurant to get her attention and greet her with a hug and a squeal. Don't do this to an Acquaintance . . . it will just make you both look and feel ridiculous. You can ask her to borrow small things like a pencil or paper, but never lip gloss or money for the Diet Coke machine. You can do an after school project with her, but you can't dish about your crush or go shopping together.

Another Acquaintance-identifier is the situational comforter. If you find yourself crying in the school bathroom because your crush just pointed out that you had toilet paper stuck to your shoe, The Acquaintance just might be able to come to the rescue. If she comes in and sees you crying, she'll probably feel compelled to ask you what happened and offer you a tri-fold paper towel from the stainless steel dispenser for your running mascara. She might offer some small condolence like "I'm sorry" or "It'll be okay" and pat you on the shoulder. Anything more than this, like a hug or a literal "shoulder to cry on" would instantly move The Acquaintance to friend status. And this makes The Acquaintance good to have around. She's kind of a friend-in-training. She could definitely wind up becoming a true friend.

The Herd

There is a time in every girl's life when she feels certain that all boys are all gross and nasty—usually around first or second grade. This is about this same time that boys are convinced that girls are stupid and have cooties. During the early elementary years, boys and girls have nothing to do with each other. They will play on opposite ends of the playground, call each other names and react meanly if they find themselves in too close proximity of the opposite sex. This is the time in life when boys and girls begin to cluster together in "girls only" or "boys only" groups. We'll call this "the huddle years." During the huddle years, boys and girls realize how much they enjoy hanging out with those of their same gender. This is important stuff to remember because it has lasting repercussions later in life. Fast forward to high school, college, or beyond. Girls and boys, even though they are now wildly attracted to *each other*, *still* like to huddle together. We believe that this learned behavior from early in life is directly responsible for our first real girl relationship, The Herd.

It's odd to call The Herd a relationship since there are so many girls involved, but we'll do it anyway. The Herd is defined as a large grouping of girls that travel in a flock or pack and share a singular common interest. (By large group we mean no less than a seven or eight and sometimes found in numbers upwards of twenty!) This doesn't necessarily mean that all the members of The Herd have a close personal relationship with each other. It just means that they like doing the same thing. Mall shopping, concerts, movies, sleepovers, an overwhelming love of sugar-free nonfat White Chocolate Mochas at Starbucks, and getting their ears pierced are all perfect excuses for a bunch of self-sufficient girls to get together and form a Herd. Maybe they do their hair or apply some makeup. Maybe they have a common love of a certain heartthrob of the moment. Could be simply to get all chatty with each other over the latest gossip.

Uncontrollable giggling is usually known to occur spontaneously in The Herd and last for much longer than it should. Anytime more than eight girls get together, there is a noticeable increase in noise and high-pitched laughter. You will also frequently hear the words "whatever," "like," and "no way," usually all at once. Knowing some of the characteristics of The Herd may help to explain one of the great mysteries that every single guy in the world puzzles over . . . why girls go to the bathroom together.

It should be noted that boys are Herd-killers. The Herd will quickly dissipate if boys are inserted into the mix. It's not designed to function with males present because it truly operates as a safe place for girls to be themselves, all silly and whatnot and doing girl-type things. When a guy shows up and finds himself caught up in the middle of The Herd, it will cause dissension within. One girl will inevitably start to flirt with the boy, other girls will then roll their eyes, and the more shy of the group will just clam up and giggle a lot. This breaks up The Herd because they are no longer focused on the thing that brought them together in the first place. You can't discuss the hotness of Ashton Kutcher with some boy present. Like, no way! Estrogen is the common thread in this festival of girly-ness. An "Este-fest," if you will. Because the Este-fest is all about being all girl. The Herd doesn't ever discuss politics or literature or the environment. Girls join Herds to learn about calorie counting and who broke up and who started dating this week.

All girl types can be found in a Herd because The Herd is universal to all. It's the one place where many different types of girls can agree on one thing. A First Chair and a Diva can certainly agree that the latest Brad Pitt movie is a must-see. But just like every pack of wild animals, there's always a leader. If there is no leader providing a clear sense of direction (like which stores are the coolest places to shop or which movie to see), the pack will disintegrate rather quickly. Leave it up to The Diva, The Overachiever, or The

Drama Queen to be out in front of The Herd, making the plans and calling the shots. And calling the shots. Poets, Rock Chicks, and Girlfriends don't participate as often in The Herd activities because they tend to be loners, slightly anti-social, or permanently affixed to their boyfriends.

The cool thing about The Herd is that it's also a place to meet new friends. The Herd's size tends to come from the core group inviting their other friends from their after school job or church or neighborhood. And because of the common purpose of the group, it's easy to form new friendships from new girls in the group. And so, The Herd grows.

The Herd, when fully alert and active, can be a frightening force of nature. Not much can stop a wild pack of girlies with a single destination in mind. It's best to stay out of their way lest you get trampled underfoot. Now following a Herd, on the other hand, can be quite entertaining. Be sure to follow at a safe distance, but close enough to see and observe all that goes on. You will learn a lot from following The Herd, including some of the mystery that is woman. But you won't learn all their secrets, so don't even try. Just enjoy the spectacle for what it is.

The Triangle
(The Cult of Personality)

Most girl relationships are fairly easy to spot. Except for the elusive Triangle relationship. We think it's somewhat like a mini-Herd. The Triangle relationship usually consists of three girls who, to the outside observer, all appear to be good friends. But looks are deceiving, especially with The Triangle. This particular relationship consists of one central figure (who we will call Number 1) and two secondary participant friends (Number 2 and Number 3). They hang out together at school, do things together, and appear to share several common interests. Anyone would assume that they are as tight as the Three Musketeers. But they have a dirty little secret and we're going to uncover it. Ready? Girls Number 2 and Number 3 are not really friends. In fact, they wouldn't consider hanging out, just the two of them, without girl Number 1 being present. The reason for the friendship is Number 1 and without Number 1 there is no friendship at all.

We know this may sound strange, so here's an example. Let's take The Athlete, The Airhead, and The Mathlete. The Athlete will be girl Number 1 and The Airhead and The Mathlete are girls 2 and 3. So, The Airhead, in her ever changing desire to figure out who she is, decides that she should be a soccer player because being more athletic will make her more desirable to the guys. She becomes pals with The Athlete so that some of her natural sports ability might rub off on her. The Mathlete, who loves competition and testing the limits of her abilities, discovers that she too has those same things in common with The Athlete, and they start to hang out and do things together. The Athlete loves both of her new friends. Teaching rudimentary soccer skills to The Airhead is both fun and funny (a lot of tripping goes on). Sitting around retelling and hearing of past competitive victories with The Mathlete gives The Athlete quite a rush. See? Both girls are drawn to the central figure and become legitimate friends with her for very different reasons. Then the fateful day comes when The Athlete invites both of her new friends to hang out after school. The Mathlete and The Airhead would have never guessed that they would be hanging out together, but there they are. These are the same two girls who might sit in the same classroom, one of them furiously scribbling shorthand notes on every word the teacher says and making flashcards with which to test herself, while the other one spends the class doodling jumbo flowers on the back of her spiral notebook or picking at the split ends of her bleach blonde hair while staring at a smudge on the chalkboard just to the left of the teacher's head. These two girls couldn't be more different, yet here they are, hanging out together with their new Athlete friend. The more they do things together, the less strange it seems, until they are quite comfortable as a trio.

But what if the The Athlete, being the central character in our example, moves to Ohio with her family (not that she'd *want* to move to *Ohio* . . .)The Airhead and The Mathlete will begin to drift apart. They no longer share the same connection they once did. Now all that remains of their friendship is a few shopping-mall photo-booth picture-strips of the three of them together. This is how The Triangle relationship works . . . or doesn't work—depending on how you want to look at it. So our lesson today is that it takes three sides to make a triangle. But only two sides equals, um . . . an "X" or maybe train tracks which would look a little something like I I. Two sides could also make a teepee shape, which we can't seem to figure out how to do on this computer. Anyway, it doesn't really matter.

The Dog/Owner relationship

Now we know what you must be thinking, and if *you're* thinking what *we're* thinking, it would certainly be accompanied by the infectious chorus to the Baha Men's classic song, "Who Let The Dogs Out?" Take a moment and let it sink in. Is that song stuck in your head yet? Good. Now with that song ringing in your ears, read on friends. You must be thinking "The Dog/Owner relationship? Sounds mean. . . . Sure, this sounds kind of scary and/or mean, but honestly, this is a type of girl relationship that does exist. And, in our relentless quest to unravel the female mind, we feel obligated to you, the reader, to bring this relationship to light. Are we right? Of course, we are. Now we'll admit that this is a somewhat rare relationship, but chances are that you yourself know someone who is in The Dog/Owner relationship. (Maybe it's you?) This is how it works. There are two girls and they are friends. They can appear to be best friends or casual friends.

There's nothing about them that will particularly puzzle you or raise an alarm. But upon closer examination, you start to realize some startling facts.

First Fact: One girl always walks slightly in front of the other. They never switch places. It is always the same girl out in front and the other following closely behind. Maybe the girl out in front has longer legs or a tendency to walk faster? Wrong. The girl out front is The Owner. She is the boss, the leader of the friendship. She is the one to make the plans, break the plans, call the shots, make the shots, and take credit for the shots. She sets the tone for the friendship. If on a given Friday night The Owner wants to go to see the ballet perform while The Dog secretly wishes to see a touring production of the Blue Man Group, it is almost certain that the evening will be filled with tiptoe twirling and crouching and leaping instead of three blue-faced guys banging on tubes with shoe leather. Nine times out of ten, The Owner gets her way. In some cases, ten out of ten. It could be that she is more confident. Could be that she is cooler or more hip. Let's be honest, The Owner could be smarter, or more savvy, or more sophisticated, or more elegant, or more outspoken, or more diplomatic, or more popular, or funnier, or richer, or prettier, or more whatever than the other girl. It could be one or more of those things or maybe even things we couldn't think of. But no matter the reason, The Owner is the dominant person in this type of relationship.

Before you go jumping to conclusions and think that The Owner is mean and manipulative there is another fact that you should know. Second Fact: The Dog likes it this way. Now if any of you are offended by the use of the term "Dog," we mean no disrespect. We don't mean "Dog" as if to comment on this girl's looks, for after all, The Dog in our scenario might be quite beautiful. Even ravishing. Even spectacularly stunning. Most guys might even consider her a *hot* dog. No, we must look at The Dog/Owner relationship as an allegory or possibly even a paradox. After all, dogs are a man's best friend, are they not?

As we were saying, The Dog enjoys this relationship immensely and finds great satisfaction in it. She enjoys fulfilling her end of this unspoken bargain and playing the part of the sidekick. It's almost like Batman and Robin, if we were to use an all-male analogy at this point. Batman is smarter, braver, and stronger than Robin. Batman also has pointy ears on his hood while Robin does not. But where would Batman be without his "boy wonder" Robin? He would probably be caught up in some trap that the Joker or the Penguin had set for him. The point is that Robin was always there to help Batman out, just like The Dog in The Dog/Owner relationship. The Dog always looks up to The Owner, and The Owner appreciates the camaraderie of The Dog. So why does this relationship seem to work? It is because both The Dog and The Owner complement each other nicely. Where one is weak, the other is strong and visa versa.

There is one more fact about The Dog/Owner Relationship that you should know. Third Fact: Neither The Dog nor The Owner fully realize or recognize the roles they play in their friendship. And this is a good thing, for if The Owner truly realized that her friend, The Dog, would do anything she wished or suggested, The Owner would begin to not respect her or take her for granted or possibly even begin to dislike her. And if The Dog were to realize that she was always the fol-lower, she may become resentful and believe that her friend, The Owner, does not take her seriously. Even though this relationship is a delicate balance of trust and ignorance, The Dog/Owner relationship is almost always a mutually rewarding friendship.

Nemesis

Ah ha! No, we don't know why we said that. The word "nemesis" just sounds like a word that should be followed by an *Ah ha!* The

Nemesis is a dark and tricky relationship that can actually appear shiny and wonderful. As best we can tell, there are two main characteristics of The Nemesis.

The first characteristic of The Nemesis is that she is your friend. This is a girl who runs in your circle of friends and is usually a School Friend or possibly even a Sista (What's a Sista? Read on and you will find out . . .). She is a girl who you want to be but aren't. Or she the girl who wants to be you and isn't. The Nemesis wants to be smarter than you, more popular than you, more athletic than you, have a better boyfriend than you . . . and wants to be your friend at the same time. She wants to hang out with you all the time, but secretly wants to beat you at every possible opportunity. If you run for Student Council President, she will either run against you or secretly plot your ruin. You will both try out for the same part on the school play. One thing we've noticed is that The Nemesis always wants to win, but never does. It's just a constant power struggle to be #1.

The second characteristic of The Nemesis is that she is the exact same Girl Type that you are. If you are a Drama Queen, she is a Drama Queen also. If you are a Poet, she is a Poet. If you are The Athlete, so is she. Neither of you can help what type of girl you are, but you find it's difficult to both exist together in the same group of friends. You both want to be known for who you are, but there seems to be two of you, and this creates a constant tension.

Now don't be confused. The Nemesis is not your enemy, but actually your friend. If you have an enemy (and we hope you don't), she is a girl who you'd want to stay far away from and she would want to stay far away from you. Enemies are mean and spiteful. They say terrible things about each other and do terrible things to each other. You wouldn't normally like each other at all. If you do have someone who you think is your enemy and don't know what to do, we have some advice for you. Get out your Bible and read Matthew 5:43–48 and try out what it says. You'll be surprised at the results. Enough for now about enemies and back to The Nemesis. The Nemesis is different because you do like each other and are in proximity to each other, but find it difficult to take up the same space. The good thing about having a Nemesis is that even for the added bit of tension she brings to your life, she can make your life a whole lot more interesting and certainly never boring. The Nemesis is like a surprise rainstorm during a picnic; she can be a mild inconvenience but also refreshing and fun. *Ah ha!*

Campfire Girls

It's summer and you're headed to camp for a week. Sounds like fun, but there's a problem. Your parents have sent you to an all-girl, smart kids camp again this year. Okay, it doesn't have to be a smart kids camp. It could be an all-girl sports camp, a church camp, or any type of camp for girls, for that matter. The thing that *is* the matter is that you don't know anyone else at this camp. No one. Every single person there will be a stranger to you, and you will be a stranger to everyone else. This might seem like a quite a bummer to you as you are sitting on the bus (surrounded by strangers) with your sleeping bag rolled up on your lap as you stare out the window at the trees whizzing by. You probably begin to feel more and more homesick as the bus pulls you farther and farther from home. In your head you know that camp will be fun, but your face is telling a different story. Don't be afraid, lonely lady, because we are here to remind you that something great awaits you at this camp full of strangers. It is the girl-friendship known as the Campfire Girls!

Campfire Girls are friends who become your friends due to an event or situation where you are thrown together, just like summer camp. It is a phenomenon of friendships that happen when a world full of strangers collide and are forced to be together in one place for a limited amount of time. In order to not feel lonely or left out, everyone is forced into hyper-fast, friend-making relationship building. Sort of like a friendship sprint race.

Within minutes of arriving, everyone starts with a flurry of introductions, wandering around to find assigned cabins, meeting your cabin-mates, unpacking, and getting settled in for the week. There is constant small talk with anyone and everyone around you. In a matter of hours after arriving, you know now dozens of girls' names, where they are from, how many brothers and sisters they have, if they have pets, the pets' names, and any interests and hobbies they have. It is one of the fastest information downloads known to man. Faster than this old computer we're typing on—that's for sure. Within three hours, you're no longer homesick. Instead, you're looking forward to a great week with your new Campfire Girl friends.

Camps are one of the fastest friendship building factories ever. The week progresses and you feel more and more comfortable with these new friends. As is normal with any new and growing friendships, you will quickly learn that you get along better with certain girls than others. By the end of the week, you have found a handful of really close friends, who seem like lifelong friends you've known for years and years. Such is the Campfire Girls phenomenon.

On Friday night at the big final bonfire (or campfire . . . you now have figured out where we got the name) there you sit, arm-in-arm with your closest Campfire Girl friends, singing songs and eating charred marshmallows with melted chocolate running down your chin. It is the happiest time in your life. This is soon to be followed by what seems to be the saddest time in your life, which happens, without fail, the next morning. There you stand, with the your dusty old sleeping bag under one arm and tears pouring down your face as you say goodbye to your best Campfire Girl friends and wait for the bus that has come to take you back home. You don't want to leave, but as you say your goodbyes, you make pinky promises to email or call every day and that you will always be friends for-ever. For-e-ver.

This, of course, does not usually happen. For several weeks after returning home, you *do* email and call your best Campfire Girls with fierce regularity, intent to stay close friends always. But after those few weeks, life starts to return to normal. You start hanging out with your regular friends and enjoying the rest of the summer together. By the time school starts back up again, the promised communication has dwindled to barely a trickle. By Christmas it has stopped alto-gether. And that's okay because it's only six more months until sum-mer camp, where you'll meet a whole new batch of Campfire Girls and the whole thing starts all over again.

By the way, becoming a Campfire Girl friend doesn't only happen at summer camps. It can happen when you're on vacation with your family, at youth retreats, Governor's School, math competitions, All-city orchestra rehearsals, or anywhere else where you are stuck with a bunch of strangers for a short amount of time. Remember not to worry and have fun because you will most likely find and become friends, if only for a while, with some other Campfire Girls.

School Friends

Now we come to a more long-lasting and viable type of girl relation-ship. These relationships are formed over a longer period of time and are more stable and reliable than say, Campfire Girls. These are School Friends. We're not pulling any surprises on you with this type of girl friend and, just like the name would suggest, these are the friends that are made at school. It doesn't matter whether you are in junior high, high school, or college. School Friends are School Friends no matter where you are in school and all the same rules will apply. Older people, like your parents, will refer to School Friends with cornball expressions like "peer group" or "my kid's friends," but these are your friends. Your *real* friends. These are the people you ride to school with, eat lunch with, study with, hang out, and work with. Your everyday friends.

Now don't get School Friends confused with The Herd. The Herd is much bigger than your group of School Friends and is made up with many girls who aren't really School Friends . . . but actually girls who are closer friends than Acquaintances but not as close as School Friends. Make sense? The Herd can number upwards of twenty people or so while the School Friends are usually between five and eight people. The difference is that you only do things *occasionally* with The Herd while your School Friends you do stuff with every single day. They become your inner circle of closest friends. In all probability, your "Best Friend" (BF) or "Sista" (Sista) is among your School Friends, but we will get to that later.

So how do girls become involved with this group of comrades that are known as the School Friends? In our attempts to satisfy your curiosity, we must turn to a proven mathematical formula known as "The Solidarity=Camaraderie theorem." The Solidarity=Camaraderie theorem is G+SD=GT+#SGTA=SF. Sound confusing? Not really. The Solidarity=Camaraderie theorem breaks out like this: Girl plus Self Discovery equals a Girl Type plus the number of Same Girl Types Available equals School Friends. Okay, okay . . . another way of saying it is this. When a girl figures out who she is, what she likes, and what makes her tick, she tends to gravitate toward other girls with whom she identifies. They find that they are more comfortable with other girls who think like they do, dress like they do, and act like they do. As these girls become better and closer friends, and share the same experiences, their trust in each other grows. This results in becoming School Friends.

You may remember our discussion about Girl Types like First Chair and The Rock Chick and how they tend to only hang out with other girls of their own type. Well, we will let you in on a little secret.

All girls have this tendency, regardless of Girl Type—and that is okay. Who wouldn't be more comfortable hanging around people who share the same interests, come from the same background, or have the same ideas and beliefs? This is normal stuff. But hold on. If you're reading this and realize that you have School Friends made up of a wide variety of different Girl Types, that's cool, too, of course. There are exceptions to these rules, and it is quite okay to have School Friends who aren't your exact same Girl Type. In fact, there is a whole lot of beauty in diversity and having good School Friends of different races, backgrounds, interests, and Girl Types and can be a very rewarding thing.

If you are still unsure about who exactly are your School Friends, take out a piece of paper and write down the answers to the following quiz:

1. List the girls you eat lunch with every day.

2. List the girls who you pass notes to during school hours.

3. List the girl(s) who share a locker with you.

4. List the girls who are in three or more of your classes.

5. List the girls who participate in your favorite after school activity.

6. List the girls who you talk on the phone to or email at least once every week.

7. List the girls who have stayed over at your house in the last month (or at whose house you have stayed over in the last month).

8. List the girls who you ride to school with.

9. List the girls who you secretly tell which guy you currently think is hot or like.

10. List the girls who have seen you cry.

Now look through this list of girls and circle the names of the girls who appear more than three times. Done? Now take a look at the names you've circled. These are, without a doubt, your School Friends. This is your group, your gang, your team. You are tight and stick up for each other. You help each other out and will maintain the peace and integrity of School Friends at all costs. There is safety in numbers, and it is your School Friends who can provide you with a sense of well being and belonging. School Friends tend to know a lot about you due to daily proximity. They know what you eat for lunch and what class you flunked and which t-shirt is your favorite. But they also know your dreams and your fears and the one thing that can always make you cry.

So no matter who your School Friends are, have a great time with them, make the most out of and enjoy your friendship with them because something is coming that will, in all likelihood, change this group of friends for good. You know what it is. You are looking forward to it and dreading it all at the same time. Graduation. High school and college graduation are events that tend to alter the course of School Friends forever. Think about the inscriptions that you used to write in your School Friends' yearbooks when you were a Sophomore or a Junior. "See you next year." "Stay COOL this summer ;)" "Hugs not Drugs." "Only 1 more year . . . and we're OUTTA HERE!" You know, stuff like that. But when you're a Senior, all that changes. Instead you are writing stuff in your School Friends' yearbooks that sounds eerily like the promises you made to your Campfire Girl friends at the end of summer camp. Promises that will be easier made than kept.

Don't worry though. You will still keep in contact with some of your School Friends. Some you may go to college with. Some you will become roommates with after college. But chances are you will drift away from many of your School Friends as you continue on in life. Oh, and as for the Solidarity=Camaraderie theorem . . . if you haven't already figured it out, we made that up.

The Little Sister Syndrome

Oh, yeah, a quick side note on School Friends. We wanted to bring your attention to a particular relational situation that can occur with School Friends. It is known as The Little Sister Syndrome. This may sound like a very serious problem and something that may require prompt medical attention, but it is actually a good thing, especially if you are a little sister. This syndrome occurs to girls who are the biological little sister of either an older brother or sister, who is no more than two or three years older. This means you will be attending the same high school or possibly college as your older sibling. If your older brother or sister is cool and has cool friends, you may be able to reap the benefits via The Little Sister Syndrome.

The Little Sister Syndrome happens when the friends of your older brother or sister come to know you as the little sister of their good friend. They may start to be nice to you and say hello to you in the halls and may even let you eat lunch with them (but don't hold your breath). If you're really lucky, they may even invite you to do stuff with them outside of school, on occasion. Maybe. When this sort of thing happens, take advantage of it. When your friends start to notice that upperclassmen pay attention to you and are nice to you, the girls in your own class will think you're pretty darn cool. And let's be honest. It *is* pretty cool. But don't for a second begin to think that these friends of your older brother or sister are your *real* friends. Remember, this is only The Little Sister Syndrome. You know who your *real* friends are. (See School Friends.)

Sistas

Imagine a target with a bull's eye in the middle. There are three rings leading in to the bull's eye. The largest, outside ring is The Herd. The second, next largest ring is the School Friends. The smallest ring that encompasses the bull's eye is the Sistas. Sistas sound like and seem like real-life sisters. Having a Sista doesn't mean that you share one or more biological parents, but there are some eerie coincidences to actual sisters. If you do have a real, genetic sister, pay special attention because some of this may freak you out. The following ten things are shared by both real-life sisters and Sistas.

1. You can argue, bicker, and fight with your Sistas over both big and small things, but you always make up quickly and resume with normal life. The next day you won't even remember that you fought or argued at all.

2. You share clothes with your Sistas. Often. There is an unspoken rule that Sistas can borrow and wear any clothes from your closet as long as they are returned within one week. This is especially good because this Sista rule instantly doubles your wardrobe.

3. You may actually call your Sista's mother by the title of Mom. For some odd reason, Sistas are able to bypass the proper titles of "Mrs. Smith" or "Mrs. Jones" and go straight to the "Mom." Mothers of Sistas actually like this and prefer to be called Mom by their daughter's Sista friends and may even start to refer to *them* as "honey," "sugar," "sweetheart," or "baby." Why this is, we have no idea. It is like some strange female social order that allows for this type of mixed-up talk.

4. You often eat dinner with your Sista's family and your Sistas will eat dinner with your own family. This family meal-swapping doesn't stop with the occasional school night, studying-together-type of meal, but can extend into weekends and, yes, even holidays. A sure-fire way to know who your Sistas are is if you are asked to eat Thanksgiving dinner with a friend and both her mom and your own mom think that's cool, you're in.

5. You are not afraid to sleep in the same bed with your Sistas. This is not a strange or weird thing for Sistas. They are such close friends that it is almost the same thing as having to share a bed or a bedroom with a real-life sister. But we will warn you, this is not the same for guys. No way. Never. Under no circumstance will any guy

be forced to sleep in the same bed next to another guy. (Save being in a poor rock and roll band and stuffing six fellas into one hotel room.) But normally it's bad enough to have to sleep in the same *room* with another guy, but it is never ever tolerable to actually sleep in the same bed. Even if the bed is twenty feet long and twenty feet wide, one guy will get to sleep in the bed and the other guy will gladly (and thankfully) sleep on the floor. This is just the way it is with guys. Sistas are different though.

6. You don't have to have something interesting to talk about with your Sistas. Sistas can get together just to watch TV or do crossword puzzles. There is not a talking requirement for Sistas. You hang with each other simply because you just prefer to be in the same room with her. Silence or talk is just fine—either way. Of course, when it is time to talk, you share all your deepest secrets that are shared with no one else.

7. You are invited to go on family vacations with your Sistas. This is another sure and foolproof sign that you are Sistas.

8. You are having a piano recital, starring in the school play, or competing for the state championship in soccer (or any other important event in your life), and you look out in the crowd and see your Sistas waving and cheering for you. But wait, there's more. Your Sista's *parents* are there, too, cheering you on. (Don't worry, so are your real parents.)

9. You don't get jealous of your Sista's other friends. A Sista can hang out or go to a party with other people, and you don't get mad or resentful about it. The true Sistas are not threatened by or jealous of other people but are secure with themselves and the Sistahood. This is because Sistas have proven themselves over time and you trust your Sistas.

10. You will tell your Sistas that you love them. To their face. This is another no-no for guys.

11. It is almost like you didn't have a choice in the matter of these your Sistas. If you stop and think about it, it is almost like you didn't choose who your Sistas would be, it just seemed to *happen*.

These Sista friends are your two or three closest friends. You know that you can be honest and say what you think and so can they. Even if your feelings get hurt, this is easily forgiven and you go right on being Sistas. The cool thing is that you don't really have any unrealistic expectations of your Sistas and you don't require much of them at all. Since there is little pressure put upon another Sista, it tends to be the most natural and enjoyable type of girl relationship that exists and has the potential to last a very long time. You may not believe us, but we think that Sistas are the girl friends who in ten years you will still keep in contact with, no matter where life takes you. Sistas are usually lifelong friends. That's pretty cool.

The BF

At last we finally arrive at the bull's eye. The crown jewel, the queen mother, the zenith, the very top and highest order of relationship a female could ever know (outside of God and future husband, of course). Ladies and gentlemen, it is our distinct pleasure to introduce you to the ever-ascendant girl-friendship known as the . . . B-E-S-T-F-R-I-E-N-D. That's right. The Best Friend. The BF. Now unlike some of these other girl relationships and friendships, there should be zero guesswork in determining your very Best Friend. In fact, you know exactly who she is so why don't you take a moment and write her name in the blank we have provided especially for you.

_____

(a.k.a. Best Friend)

It would be presumptuous of us to pretend that we have any specific knowledge about your Best Friend, like how you found each other and became Best Friends. But we will take some time to make some observations of what we have personally witnessed, from afar, between girl Best Friends. We should also let you know that we have never had the opportunity to get too close or even right in the middle of girl Best Friends. No guy has, really. That would be sort of like trying to get close to a mother lion and her cubs. If you did, you can bet that you'd be hurtin' for certain. The same goes for girl Best Friends. That is sacred ground between girls. Boys are not welcome.

From what we can gather, there are countless ways that girls become Best Friends. You may have grown up from a very early age with a girl from next door and over the years you became inseparable until at last it was obvious to you both that you were Best Friends. You also may have found your Best Friend in another way a bit later in life. You might have been hanging at the mall with The Herd and met a new girl who seemed pretty cool. After a couple of encounters with the new girl in Herd-like situations, you see her at school and ask her to eat lunch with you and your School Friends. (You can see where this is heading.) The new School Friend eventually graduates to Sista and then, possibly, to Best Friend. There are so many ways that girls arrive at Best Friends we won't venture any further guesses.

In general, Best Friend relationships are the most extreme relationships a girl can have. First there is the difficulty of the name Best Friend. To have someone you consider your *best* friend seems to imply that all other friends are worse friends. Or to put it nicely, other friends are not as good as your Best Friend. Even if that is the case, how did this friend become the best? This is yet another mystery of the female mind that requires some unraveling. It seems to us that being a Best Friend comes with a certain side effect, and that is the intensity of having expectations attached to the friendship.

There isn't a form or application to fill out in order to become Best Friends, and girls don't generally ask permission from each other to call someone their Best Friend, they just do. Best Friend-ness just happens. Now, there are some cases we've heard about when one girl calls another girl her BF, but the sentiment is not returned. When this happens, we understand that it ranks as one of the single most worst moments ever in a girl's life. Ouch. You never, ever would want to call someone your BF and for her not to return the favor. Never. It's just too horrible. But since there's no test and no application, and since becoming Best Friends just kinda happens, how do you *really* know if you ever had a best friend to begin with? Man, girls are confusing. We think there should be an official, government sanctioned "Official Best Friend" application and license. It would be sort of like getting your driver license. There could be a little pamphlet that instructs "How You Can Be The Very Best Friend" and once you studied the pamphlet, your mom would drive you downtown to a building where you'd stand in a line for thirty minutes and then take a test. If you passed, then you would get a little plastic card that said "BEST FRIENDS" and have yours and her picture on it. Then you would have proof of who your BF is. That would be such a relief, wouldn't it? If you feel the same way we do, please take this moment to write a quick letter to your Senator or Congressman and let them know how you feel about this matter. Do it for Best Friends everywhere.

Another downside to The BF is that everybody, even guys, wants to have one. It's sort of a modern rite of passage. You gotta have a Best Friend. We've even heard it being discussed, while secretly observing a Herd in conversation. Two girls will meet. After exchanging pleasantries, one will inevitably ask, "Who's your best friend?" Or one girl will sneak it in to conversation, "Julia was saying, she's my best friend, that blah . . . blah . . . blah . . . Seems to us like the ground rules need to be set up fairly quickly. As long as everyone is aware of who is best friends with whom, conversation can continue.

Unlike the Sista, The BF comes with one ugly trait. Jealousy. Because The BF is tagged the "best," she is expected to consistently perform at this level. She has to be the constant companion, the best listener, the best advice giver, the best everything. Sometimes this can be tiring, and The BF will slack on her duties. She may let an entire day go by without calling or emailing. She might forget to meet you at your locker after second period. When this happens, trouble erupts. You may start to feel like she is hanging out with someone else more than you. This is obviously not allowed since she is your BEST friend. Because she is your BF, she isn't allowed to fail. And it's hard work to be the best all the time.

But we don't mean to be negative. BFs are called the best for a reason. She's your ultimate closest friend ever. She knows the things that no one else knows. She knows how you got that scar on your left knee and why you wear yellow on Thursdays. She's the friend you miss after being apart for fifteen minutes. She's the friend you don't make plans with, because she's always in your plans. You love her fiercely and cherish the closeness you have. After all, she's the best.

* * *

Well, we weren't kidding when we said that there is combustion when you girls get together. Your relationships are quite strange to guys and as different as dog owners are from cat owners. One thing is for sure, though; your relationships certainly aren't boring. But the fun has only begun. In the next section, we will throw in a little testosterone and it's anyone's guess what will happen next. Okay, we actually know what happens next, but you probably don't. So read on.

CHAP STICK, CHAPPED LIPS AND THINGS LIKE CHEMISTRY: BOY + GIRL RELATIONSHIPS

t's a media sensation, this thing called love. The relationship between male and female has been scrutinized, hypothesized, pasteurized, and super-sized. Every poet, writer, pastor, teacher, and pet storeowner has pondered its complexities. So we thought, hey, maybe we should take a crack at it, too.

The Celebrity Crush

This crazy little thing called romantic love begins at a surprising age. Right about the time little girls put away their baby dolls for a whole new doll. Only this new doll isn't a baby, she's a woman. The perfect woman.

Back in about first grade, every girl on the planet somehow seems to become aware of another girl, a much older girl. This girl has long blonde hair with legs to match. She also has an ideal California tan that's about the same color as Barbie's Silly Putty Legs. She also has clothes–lots of clothes . . . swimwear and evening wear and beach wear and casual wear. We're not sure what this all means, we just know she has them. And to top it off, she drives a pink Corvette. We're pretty sure you know who we're talking about. Her name is Barbie and she's made of plastic. In fact, her whole world is made up of unconvincing plastic. But this doesn't stop every little girl from playing with her and becoming her friend.

Barbie is a monster hit with the post-toddler crowd, not because of who she is (a molded lump of plastic with looong legs and a pink Corvette) but because of what she symbolizes. To every little girl, Barbie is the symbol of what they might become someday—the perfect-looking girl with all the perfect things. One of Barbie's most impressive perfect things is her infamous sidekick, Ken. Ken is Barbie's husband or boyfriend, depending on how you see things. And just like her, he is dang good looking, has a lot of cool clothes, probably a nice car, too, and pecs to *die* for. These two are America's perfect couple, and most every young girl's initiation to what a boy+girl relationship looks like. Little girls are free to use their *imaginations* and create the perfect guy with the perfect manners to date their friend Barbie. None of this really matters until years after Ken and Barbie are packed away in a box in the attic and long since forgotten about. About the time when girls start to notice boys and think that it would be nice to have a boyfriend, there is a nagging sense in the back of their minds about who the perfect guy for them must be. (Why it's Ken, of course. He was the perfect guy for Barbie, so he must be the perfect guy for me.) But the perfect guy was only imaginary. A toy. This begins the development of The Celebrity Crush.

The Celebrity Crush, put simply, is an imaginary relationship that a girl makes up in her head. Someone who a girl dreams about and likes to pretend she's with in some sort of real relationship. The most obvious example of this are those hot Hollywood hunks or super cute musicians or towering sports stars whose pictures are hung up in bedrooms and school lockers. These are the pictures that are kissed goodnight like they might become real at any moment and kiss back. Basically anyone who is cute and famous can be the subject of The Celebrity Crush.

The girl with the crush, or Crusher, finds out every possibly fact she can about the guy who she has a crush on (the Crushee). She goes on the Internet to find out his birthday, how old he is, and all of his likes and dislikes. She will go see all of his movies, study and memorize his music and lyrics, or watch all of his games on TV. She will read every interview ever published with him and collect everything she can with his picture on it. The Crusher attempts to know the Crushee as much as she can without any chance of ever meeting him or speaking to him. She puts all the pieces together in her mind and invents exactly how he must *really* be like in real life. But her favorite part of The Celebrity Crush is the long hours she spends thinking about him and imagining what it would be like to spend a day together with him. What would she say to him? Where would they go and what would they do together? How would he treat her? Would he be funny? What would her friends think if they saw them together? And the list goes on and on and on . . .

But The Celebrity Crush doesn't have to be someone famous either. It could actually be a guy at school or church that is probably super good-looking and has, for whatever reason, captured the eye of the Crusher. It could even be another friend's boyfriend. No matter the situation, The Celebrity Crush will always occur only when the Crushee is out of reach of the Crusher. If the two talk at all or know each other at all, it doesn't work. The Celebrity Crush has to be someone unreachable in real life. It could be that he's older, richer, famous, or far away. People always tend to want what they can't have, and this is the one permanent rule for The Celebrity Crush.

10 Ways to recognize if you Have the Celebrity Crush:

1. You have more than 3 of his web pages bookmarked.

2. His name is written multiple times on the back of several of your spiral notebooks.

3. You don't know him well enough to pick up the phone and have a conversation with him.

4. You have developed a website for him or you moderate his fan club message board.

5. His face is the background picture for your computer desktop or cell phone.

6. You write him letters or emails about how much you like him, but you never send them.

7. You know about his current girlfriend and secretly despise her.

8. You won't admit it to yourself, but you know in your heart that he will never like you back.

9. He is the last thing you think about at night before you fall asleep as you imagine him calling out your name over and over and over again—even though he has no idea what your name is.

10. He is the first thing on your mind when you wake up; that is, unless you have slept though your alarm clock and are now an hour late for school or work, in which case you have other more important things to think about. But admit it, you're still thinking about him.

As long as The Celebrity Crush doesn't turn into an overly obsessive, psycho-stalker situation, it is quite harmless and fun. But it can't be exchanged for real life. It's cool to dream about some guy, but imaginary expectations should never be anticipated in real life. A Celebrity Crush should be recognized for what it is . . . a harmless imaginary crush. Holding out for something or someone that's only a reality in your mind can be harmful. Trust us, us regular guys could never live up to it.

The Study Buddy

Thankfully, The Celebrity Crush is the only imaginary relationship. One very real and very cool relationship between boys and girls is the Study Buddy, although it's really more of a friendship than a relationship. The Study Buddy is a guy friend, who is not unlike a School Friend or Campfire Girl in that he is a fairly casual friend or may only be a friend for a short length of time. Girls do not actively seek out The Study Buddy but become friends with him purely by proximity or circumstance. He could be a neighbor or someone she sits beside in class. She might have met him at church or at some local club or organization.

The instant she meets The Study Buddy, two things happen. First, she knows without a doubt that she is not attracted to him in any way shape or form. Now don't go jumping to conclusions and think that The Study Buddy is always an ugly guy. He could be an attractive guy for sure, but just not *her type* of attractive guy. The second thing that happens is that, though she is not attracted to him, there is a connection made. This connection usually isn't a big mind-blowing moment, merely an encounter that makes the girl think he's nice, cool, interesting, funny, thoughtful, or smart—especially for a guy for whom she holds no romantic interest.

The Study Buddy begins just like any other relationship, through a process of getting to know each other. The difference is, this process doesn't ever progress very far beyond the thing or place that both people have in common. For instance, if you happen to meet a guy whom you're not attracted to at school, this Study Buddy relationship doesn't evolve to anything outside of school. You may study together in the library, hang out at a school basketball game, or maybe even sit at the same table during lunch. But you would never hang out on the weekend together. Likewise, if you meet a guy at church who becomes your Study Buddy, you may hang out in the youth group, go to a rock and roll show with him, or sit with him during the church service, but your companionship doesn't extend outside of church stuff. If it does, he is no longer your Study Buddy but something else.

The Study Buddy may actually have a girlfriend of his own or he may be single and unattached—it doesn't matter because romance is not the reason for The Study Buddy. In fact, conversations about love do not happen with The Study Buddy because that would be too personal for this type of relationship. The reason that girls have The Study Buddy is because he is useful to the girl. Whether it is for company or someone to study with, The Study Buddy is always a good thing to have. But ladies, we must warn you about something. Always be careful with your Study Buddy, especially the unattached ones, because he very well might be interested in you as more than just a friend. Sorry to say, but guys are like this sometimes. It may be a good thing to define your friendship with your Study Buddy to make sure he knows that you aren't interested in dating him, just in case, so his feelings won't be hurt (or crushed . . . hey, maybe that's why they call it a crush . . .). Don't worry though, this is normal and happens all the time because guys like girls, whether you want them to or not.

The Outfielder

If a Study Buddy is only a little more than an acquaintance type of friend to a girl, our next guy friend is on the right track to being more than just a friend. Maybe. He is The Outfielder. To begin, The

Outfielder is attractive, even in a small or modest way, to the girl. It could even be subconscious. This is a non-negotiable fact and foundational to being or becoming The Outfielder. With this attraction, however small, things will become undeniably complicated. It is our assertion that it is impossible for guys and girls to be truly *just friends* if there is any attraction between the two on either side. If the guy is attracted to the girl, even subconsciously, there cannot truly be simple friendship. If the girl is attracted to the guy, even subconsciously, there cannot truly be simple friendship. The problem is that when a person finds the other friend to be attractive in some way, there will always be the looming question of "What If? . . ." What If we dated? What If he tried to kiss me? What If I asked her on a date? The What If question left unanswered will always bring about a sense of awkwardness, no matter how hard anyone attempts to ignore it.

And so it is with The Outfielder. The girl's primary objective for The Outfielder is to see if something more will develop with him or to see if something might develop with one of his friends. Either way, The Outfielder serves as a romantic link. A girl may have many Outfielder friends who are single or have girlfriends. The catch is that the girl will have an agenda to get to know him better and to become somewhat closer friends with him, than with say The Study Buddy. Girls like to talk to The Outfielder about who they like or who they think is hot in order to get a reaction from him. Girls treat The Outfielder like a baseball outfielder because they try to hit pop-up fly balls (in the form of questions) and see if he will catch them. They will even ask him questions about other girls to see what he will say. Do you think she's cute? Would you date her? Do you think they make a cute couple? Whatever his answer, the girl will inevitably form a complex theory on what the guy thinks and why. He may not realize she is doing this. He is probably not putting any thought into his answers, just shooting from the hip. But his answers will be studied and analyzed and then studied some more.

Generally speaking, when guys and girls begin to discuss their feelings with those of the opposite gender, they are making themselves a little susceptible to having their hearts broken. If they are able to be open and honest with each other about personal things and not get their hearts broken or feel betrayed, there is a good chance for a real relationship to develop, whether it is a romantic one or not, because there is a level of trust involved in the relationship. That's really the heart of The Outfielder relationship . . . trying things out. Sharing small parts of yourself and seeing if the other will accept you for you. The Outfielder is about taking small risks. Usually ones that are worth it.

Guys love to be The Outfielder. Guys love to play the part of The Outfielder, no matter where it leads, because it is an honor just to be included in the game.

The Backup

Next up to bat (okay, okay . . . enough with the baseball analogies . . .) is The Backup. He's a champ, maybe even our favorite. The Backup is a girl's best guy friend. He's the BF, only he's a guy. He'll never be as close to the girl as her BF, but he'll be much closer than her other guy friends. He's much higher up on the food chain than the Study Buddy or The Outfielder. But he's also a lot more complicated.

The Backup is cute, or at least you think he is, but you're really *just* friends. Just friends. Well, all right. You may have the occasional "What If?" moments with The Backup, but you sincerely view him as a friend. A confidante. A pal. You know that he is nice, funny, and thoughtful, like The Study Buddy, but you have much more in common. There is a greater connection between you two, which makes it natural to want to hang out with The Backup more often than you would The Study Buddy. After all, this is a guy who your mom knows and hugs. She asks him to stay for dinner and that makes you happy. You watch *The O.C.* or *Aqua Teen Hunger Force* together and eat Cheetoes and burp in front of each other. You can paint your toenails in front of him. He is a true friend. A cute, true friend.

How does a guy get to be a true friend to a girl? Well, probably because he listens and is caring and is funny and is cute. Those might not be all the reasons, but we don't claim to know *all* the reasons why girls and guys become friends. He is The Backup because there is a level of comfort with him that is only found in a special sort of guy. The Backup is the guy who you will go to the junior prom with if you don't happen to be asked by another guy. He'll take you to the movies on Friday night if your crush cancels on you, and he'll let you cry on his shoulder when you show up at the movies and your crush is there with someone else. Warning: Be sure that The Backup knows he is only the *backup*, though. You really don't want to lead this guy on or let him think that you're interested in him romantically. This would ruin a really good guy hang, for sure. So if The Backup knows where he stands with you, it is a good thing because he'll still treat you like a princess, no matter what. You know he will. He enjoys his role as The Backup just as much as you enjoy *having* a backup. The Backup is your stand-in boyfriend on certain occasions and will save you from unnecessary humiliation and embarrassment. He is there for you like a Sista but doesn't smell as nice.

The Pre-Chem

It is said that to have romance, you must first have chemistry. Welcome friends to the dance of pre-romance. The target is set. You know for sure who you like and you're going to go for it. The problem is, you don't have any idea what this guy thinks about you. He is your Pre-Chem, the guy who has your full and undivided attention but you're not sure if you have his . . . yet.

Have you even been at a party with a Pre-Chem and were sitting on the couch side-by-side? You might have been having a deep conversation and looking into each other's eyes as you discussed the finer points of pop music or the intrigue of your favorite author. Then it happened. His hand inadvertently brushed yours and you felt something. Something electric. You got goose bumps as all the blood in your body flushed to your face. You felt all nervous but ecstatic at the same time. You didn't know whether to scream out loud or giggle, but you managed to keep it all in and maintain your cool. Later that night, all you can think about was that his hand brushed yours. Was it a sign? Was he trying to tell you that he likes you, too? What would it be like if he actually held your hand? Your mind wanders off into the world of possibilities and it stays there until you fall asleep. When you wake up in the morning, the first thing on your mind is The Pre-Chem.

The Pre-Chem is often filled with mystery and intrigue. You are *dying* to know what he is thinking and your sole occupation is to figure it out. This will involve many other people from whom you will solicit feedback and try to gain inside information. You may ask all of your School Friends, Sistas, or Best Friend whether or not they think your Pre-Chem likes you. If they don't know, you will insist that they help you find out. As you set off to gather information and try to build a case in your mind that he does indeed like you, this is where the games are played. You may drop a book to see if he will pick it up. You might let the air out of one of your tires after school to see if he will help you change your spare. There are a whole bunch of crazy things that you girls will do to see if a Pre-Chem is interested.

Having a Pre-Chem also involves the eye-flirt. The eye-flirt is a thing that girls mainly do with their eyes. It is a certain look that they give a guy . . . not a smile but more of an invitation, with one raised eyebrow. In length, it falls somewhere between a glance and a stare, but it comes with a certain implication. It's so complex and hard to describe that we will stop trying now. But you are a girl and you know what we mean by the eye-flirt.

And on the occasion that you are able to have a good conversation with The Pre-Chem, a serious download of information occurs. This is where you try to *casually* let him know your life history in the shortest amount of time possible. Girls do this, we think, to show The Pre-Chem all their selling points in hopes that he will take the bait. And if he does take the bait, you will be . . .

Hooked

All at once you feel yourself floating high above the clouds and nothing in the world can touch you now. Your smile is more blinding than the sun. The flowers bloom and the birds sing just for you. There is peace in the world and everything is better than just okay. The guy of your dreams is now your boyfriend. You have become Hooked.

If you have a boyfriend, you know it. And he knows it, too. There has been a series of conversations that have led up to one unmistakable fact. You two are together and that is enough. When a girl and a guy get Hooked, it is a spellbinding and thrilling thing. Kind of like a magician pulling a dove out of his sleeve, you have no idea what will happen, but you can't wait to see what's next. (You kinda hope the dove spontaneously combusts.) The thing about being hooked is that it is like pretending to be married, but without living together or sex. Both Hookees have this same goal in mind, which is to see if their relationship will one day turn into marriage. This is exactly what each Hookie is thinking to themselves. In order to do that, they spend all their time together. Every possible second. They eat together, walk together, talk together, and can't stand to *not* be together. And when they're not together, they do something to be together even if they can't actually be together like write each other notes, text message each other, or talk on the phone. Ah, the phone . . .

There is a game that all Hookies play that involves the phone. At the end of a long, evening phone conversation, neither of them are willing to hang up first. The girl might say that she needs to get off the phone and go to bed. The guy will then say okay. It may go something like this:

Girl says: Okay. Good night.
Guys says: Good night. See you tomorrow.
((silence))
Girl: ((giggles)) Come on. You can hang up now.
Guy: No. You first.
Girl: No, I can't. *You* first.
((silence))
Guy: No. How about let's hang up together.
Girl: ((giggles)) Okay.
Guy: Alright then. On the count of three. Ready?
Girl: Yep
Guy: One . . .
Guy: Twooooooo . . .
Girl: ((giggles))
Guy: Threeeeeeee . . .
((silence))
Guy: Why didn't you hang up?
Girl: I *can't* hang up on you. It just feels rude . . .
Guy: Well, we'll have to hang up *sometime* . . .

Sadly, this late night phone conversation doesn't end for another ten minutes. Hookies can't figure out how to end their phone conversations. It's too awkward and weird. If this has ever happened to you, it is a sure sign that you were (or are) Hooked.

Being Hooked can be a beautiful thing. Usually and hopefully, it is a scenario where a girl and guy can be in a safe, romantic relationship with each other that might someday lead to something more.

* * *

So this is how the girl meets boy story often goes. From friend to boyfriend and maybe back again. If we've learned one thing in our study of girls and their guy relationships, it is that everyone needs to have relationships. And this isn't wrong or bad, it is right and just the way you girls and we boys were created.

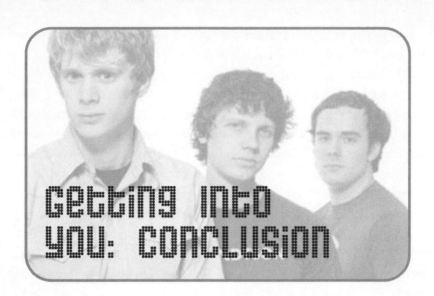

Getting Into You: Conclusion

We have almost arrived at the end of our journey through *The Complex Infrastructure Known as the Female Mind*. For the most part, we have examined the differences that comprise all the distinctive types of girls that we could think of out there. Girls certainly look different from each other and come in a variety of styles. They all have diverse personalities, from the most quiet, studious, and introverted to the loud, outgoing, and dynamic. Some girls are into music and art, some are into sports, some are into school and learning, and others are into shopping and boys, and many, many other things.

Girls can be friendly and girls can be mean. Some girls can have a positive attitude towards life while others don't have such a cheery viewpoint. Whether girls are happy or gloomy, short or tall, busy or lazy, quiet or loud . . . all of these differences are the very things that make this world of girls a little bit more beautiful, interesting, and fascinating. Diversity is something to be celebrated and embraced, no matter what. No one wants to live in a world where everything and everyone is the same. We don't. That would be boring and way too predictable.

But for all the differences of the female gender, there is one thing that we haven't really discussed yet and that is the stuff that *all* girls share, regardless of what makes them unique. Sure there are physical characteristics that all girls share, but that is hardly what we're talking about here. Though girls may think, act, and look radically different, there are some central things that are the same for every single girl, all the time, without exception. Girls have needs. This may sound like a bad thing . . . that girls have needs—but it's not. Needs are normal. Even guys have needs. These are requirements that go beyond needing air to breathe and food to grow. Of all the girls who we have met, every single one has at least three basic needs, and those are to be known, to be accepted, and to be loved.

All girls want to be known—known for who they really are. No matter what different type of girl, they want to be recognized for who they really are and not for some made up, false identity. Sure there are girls who pretend to be something they're not—actually most people in general do this a little bit—but at the end of the day, it's easier and a whole lot more enjoyable to simply be true to who you are. Girls, whether they realize it or not, want people to know them for who they are and for the things they do. Girls want to make an impact and a difference in this world. They want to be successful. This doesn't necessarily mean that girls only want to be famous with their names in lights or to discover the cure for cancer or to feed the world's starving children or to become the best president ever (though they stand a better chance to do these things than guys simply because girls are smart). No, girls desire make an impact and difference in the world because they care and that is the way they were created. Yes, even The Rock Chicks. We have yet to meet a single girl who truly didn't care about anything at all. All girls are completely unique individuals with something exceptional to offer the world.

This next need that all girls share is kind of ironic because while girls want to stand out and be recognized, they also need to fit in. But ironic doesn't mean strange. Girls need to belong, to be part of a community of other people who accept them for who they are and who value them for who they are. And we're not talking about simply being tolerated by others. There is a big difference between being accepted and being tolerated. Being accepted into a group of other people means that a girl will have a relationships with other people and that her role in this group is vital and necessary. Girls were not created to be by themselves. And no one is, for that matter. When a girl finds herself in good relationships with others, she will feel safe and secure. Feeling safe and protected and being a part of a community are ways in which we find some measure of comfort and stability in this world.

And lastly, girls need to be loved. Sure, this sounds a bit like being accepted, but there's a lot more to being loved than just acceptance. For a girl, to be loved means that she finds herself on the receiving end of good things that she cannot control or earn. Love is an act of someone's intention and doesn't just happen. You can't make someone love you if they don't want to. When we talk about love, we're talking about much more than a boy holding a girl's hand for the first time. (That might be the beginnings of something that might someday become love, but it is probably no more than simple affection. Give it a bit of time and you will find out.) Girls will look for love from their family, their girl friends, their boy friends, and sometimes they even hope for it from strangers. But for a girl to find love, real and genuine love, these are the things she will find: kindness, understanding, generosity, respect, thoughtfulness, empathy, friendliness, helpfulness, concern, care, support, and affection. Anything short of these things, and you can bet that what she has found is something less than love. Love involves sacrifice on the other person's part, so ladies, don't settle for anything less than the real thing or you will be highly disappointed and maybe even hurt.

So these are three things that all girls of every style and type share and have in common. The problem with these needs is that it is impossible for all of them to be met completely, all the time, here in this world. We don't know of any girl who has always felt that they were known for who they are, found complete acceptance, and felt really loved from their families, friends, or boys all the time. The reason for this is that people are imperfect and, while we all may have good intentions, we will fail each other often. There is no way around this fact. But while things may seem a little hopeless for girls and their common needs, we have written this final little survival guide for you, our female friends.

Survival Guide

We believe that no matter who you are, you can be known, accepted, and loved. We believe and know that there is God who actually made you and knows all your crazy quirks. If God created all things that exist, he also created you. He made you to be the person you are, whether you are The Athlete, First Chair, Vanilla Pudding, or any of the other nine plus types of girls. You are completely unique, you have your own identity, and you were made for a good reason. We might not know what you were made/created to be and do, but God knows. If you ever feel that you don't know what your deal is, just ask God. He will answer your questions and show you the importance of your life. He sure has for us.

Not only has God made you unique and knows you completely, quirks and all, but he accepts you for who you are. You might rest a little easier knowing that you can't live up to what God deserves or asks of you, but he accepts you anyway. And what does God ask of us, you may be wondering? He simply wants us to love him. Even if you don't know how to love God, he will help you with that. Again, all you need to do is ask. Since he knows our imperfections and weaknesses, he is more than happy to fill in the gaps for us and to help us be more than we can imagine. God sees you as his daughter, and you have a place in his family. He doesn't just do this because he's God and he's obligated to be nice. God truly cares for you and wants to protect you. He wants to give you strength and keep you safe. This doesn't mean that bad stuff won't ever happen, but it does mean that he will carry you through hard times and celebrate with you in good times. God makes a place for us and looks over us, and even though we can never do anything to warrant it, he receives us for who we are. That is what real acceptance looks like.

There is one last thing in our survival guide for you to know and that is the unconditional love that God has for you. He knows your needs, your faults, and your shortcomings, and decided that he loves you anyway. He loves you so much that he made an ultimate sacrifice on your behalf. Think of all your failures and your flaws. Not a pretty picture, huh? Those things, though they aren't much fun to think about, are the things that God has made up for through the life of his son Jesus. God sent Jesus here to earth to live a perfect life, free of failure and flaw. Jesus was innocent and blameless but in the end was brutally beaten and killed on our behalf for our failures and flaws. That is the sacrifice that gave us a place in God's family and makes us perfect in God's eyes. You will never experience such drastic love by any other person than Jesus. God, through Jesus, makes the unlovable like you and like us completely lovable.

These three things are what girls (and guys) need, and God is there to meet these needs. And in meeting these needs, he has also given you a new identity. Don't be mistaken. You could be the most popular Homecoming Queen ever or the smartest Mathlete or the raddest Rock Chick or the most normal Vanilla Pudding or the most expressive Drama Queen, but the single most important identity you could ever have is to be the completely known, accepted, and loved daughter of God. That is your one true identity and is something that can never be taken from you. No matter who and where you are in your life, whether you feel like a piece of discarded chewing gum stuck under a chair or have the greatest, most charmed life that you could ever have imagined, remember who and what you really are. School can be hard and people can be ruthless, but we know that God will hold you and carry you through whatever things you face in life. You're not good enough to deserve God's favor (and neither are we), no matter how hard you try, but he gives you his favor anyway. So live in light of who you really are . . . a daughter of God who has been made perfect in the eyes of God and who loves you unconditionally. He has big things in store for your life.

We hope you have enjoyed your journey into *The Complex Infrastructure Known as the Female Mind*. It was certainly fun for us and we hope it was for you, too.